Praise for *Agile Now*

'A practical look at what it means to be agile and how this isn't just for the techies among us. Straightforward guidance on the theory, tools and, most importantly, the themes of mindset and culture were handled with humour and honesty.'

Amanda Hickey, Head of Business Change and Innovation, Solera-Autodata

'An easy read for anyone curious about how agile can be applied to any business environment. It's more than enough to get anyone up to speed and it doesn't over complicate the subject.'

David Daiches, COO and Co-Founder, INSHUR

'Agile is an extremely lucrative market, and this book unlocks its secrets for just the cost of a takeaway pizza. This humorous, easy-to-read book upskills its readers and entertains them as it educates them on the project management method, which is all the rage in large and small companies up and down the land. It brings its readers from being on the outside to very much on the inside for this much sought-after skill.'

Gerry McLaughlin, owner, www.ITContractor.com

'Agile is perhaps the most misunderstood, misused and confusing term in project management today but here, finally, is a book that talks plainly and simply about agile - I especially love the 'Go Agile in 15 minute' suggestions. Read it! Go agile!'

Peter Taylor, author, *The Lazy Project Manager*

'As a doctor working in the NHS for 38 years, agile would benefit doctors and managers engaged with managing the world's largest bureaucracy. It provides focus on clarity of thought with distinct aims and objectives rather than process and form which can stifle innovation and positive change.'

Professor Neil S Tolley MD FRCS DLO, Head of Otolaryngology – Head & Neck Surgery -Imperial College NHS Healthcare Trust, London, UK

Agile Now

Pearson

At Pearson, we have a simple mission: to help people make more of their lives through learning.

We combine innovative learning technology with trusted content and educational expertise to provide engaging and effective learning experiences that serve people wherever and whenever they are learning.

From classroom to boardroom, our curriculum materials, digital learning tools and testing programmes help to educate millions of people worldwide – more than any other private enterprise.

Every day our work helps learning flourish, and wherever learning flourishes, so do people.

To learn more, please visit us at **www.pearson.com/uk**

Agile Now

Your quick start
introduction to *agile*

Rob Cole

Pearson

Harlow, England • London • New York • Boston • San Francisco • Toronto • Sydney
Dubai • Singapore • Hong Kong • Tokyo • Seoul • Taipei • New Delhi
Cape Town • São Paulo • Mexico City • Madrid • Amsterdam • Munich • Paris • Milan

PEARSON EDUCATION LIMITED
KAO Two
KAO Park
Harlow CM17 9SR
United Kingdom
Tel: +44 (0)1279 623623
Web: www.pearson.com/uk

First edition published 2020 (print and electronic)

© Pearson Education Limited 2020 (print and electronic)

ISBN: 978-1-292-23200-3 (print)
        978-1-292-23201-0 (PDF)
        978-1-292-23202-7 (ePub)

British Library Cataloguing-in-Publication Data
A catalogue record for the print edition is available from the British Library

Library of Congress Cataloging-in-Publication Data
A catalog record for the print edition is available from the Library of Congress

10 9 8 7 6 5 4 3 2 1
24 23 22 21 20

Cover design by Madras

Print edition typeset in 10/14 Charter ITC Pro by SPi Global
Printed by Ashford Colour Press Ltd, Gosport

NOTE THAT ANY PAGE CROSS REFERENCES REFER TO THE PRINT EDITION

Contents

——

About the author

———

Rob is an agile coach, program manager and author with a passion for getting the best out of individuals, teams and organisations. He has a special interest in thorny challenges, especially when there are non-negotiable constraints.

Always hands-on, Rob works closely with his partners to implement innovative, best-practice based solutions and to help steer them through any choppy waters – emerging confident, fully self-sufficient and ready for the challenges ahead.

Rob promotes building on existing internal expertise – training, coaching and mentoring are all on offer. But he knows continuing to delivery business value meanwhile is an essential bread-and-butter requirement. The school of hard knocks has taught Rob that resilience and a sense of humour are vitally important too.

Rob has helped many diverse organisations in the UK, Ireland and the US, including Mobil Oil, ABN AMRO Bank, Sainsburys, Eircom, Association of British Insurers (ABI), HM Revenue & Customs and the Environment Agency, plus multiple small and medium-sized enterprises (SMEs).

Rob is the co-author of *Brilliant Project Management* and *Brilliant Agile Project Management*, both published by Pearson Business.

Publisher's acknowledgements

11 **Victor Hugo:** Victor Hugo **12** *Agile Manifesto:* ©*Agile Manifesto* Copyright 2001: Kent Beck, Mike Beedle, Arie van Bennekum, Alistair Cockburn, Ward Cunningham, Martin Fowler, James Grenning, Jim Highsmith, Andrew Hunt, Ron Jeffries, Jon Kern, Brian Marick, Robert C. Martin, Steve Mellor, Ken Schwaber, Jeff Sutherland, Dave Thomas. **21 Yogi Berra:** Yogi Berra **43 Ty Warner:** Ty Warner **61 Manu Bennett:** Manu Bennett **103 Maya Angelou:** Maya Angelou **121 Jose Mourinho:** Jose Mourinho **10 Ken Pyne:** Ken Pyne **23 Ken Pyne:** Ken Pyne **55 Ken Pyne:** Ken Pyne **65 Ken Pyne:** Ken Pyne **87 Ken Pyne:** Ken Pyne **105 Ken Pyne:** Ken Pyne **122 Ken Pyne:** Ken Pyne

chapter 1

Let's get started

"There is one thing stronger than all the armies in the world, and that is an idea whose time has come."

Victor Hugo

Agile Now is an intentionally slim volume that aims to get to the essence of what *agile* can do for you – your job, your work and your life. Enough to get you started even if you know nothing about *agile*, and a helping hand for anyone already en route. Full coverage of what *agile* is and how it works, with guidance on adopting an *agile* mindset and embracing an *agile* culture. Plus, plenty of specific advice for getting the best results.

Please read on. The ultimate litmus test is whether *agile* works for you. Let results be your guide!

A sneak preview of Chapter 1

This is a fast-track introduction into the world of *agile* and what it can potentially offer you, including:

- **What is *agile*?**: You'll see it's much more than a buzzword – it's a way of life.

- **How can *agile* help you?**: Putting the hype to one side, what's really on offer?
- **Where to start?**: Don't worry, you need look no further as this book has everything you need.

The wonderful world of *agile*

It's no exaggeration to say that interest in *agile* has exploded over the past decade. Chances are you've already heard the rumours or even had some direct exposure. The word-of-mouth is overwhelmingly positive and the buzz around the subject is incredible at times. Many have already dived in but there are plenty of others still having a think or even not too sure what the hullabaloo is all about.

Agile isn't an overnight success story and has an excellent track record over recent years, hence the exponential growth. Admittedly it's been dogged by a bit of a reputation for being best suited to the world of technology, but it's becoming clear that it has a much wider appeal with all shapes and sizes now dipping their toes in the water. The *agile revolution* is definitely going mainstream.

The honeymoon period for *agile* is fast coming to an end and it's fair to say that not *everyone* is convinced. The pro lobby remains very strong, but disbelievers are passionate too. The prevailing expert view is that in the right hands it will help make the world into a better place, but positive effects aren't guaranteed. Get it right and the results are exceptional but it's no miracle cure.

What is *agile?*

The *agile* tag is used quite loosely at times. You'll hear generic references to the world of *agile,* comments on being *agile*, advice on going *agile,* references to *agile* tools and plenty more besides. There are even raging debates about whether *agile* is legitimately a verb, noun or an adjective. Honest. Without doubt the *agile* moniker is used loosely but we'll concentrate on it as a way of thinking, an innovative approach to getting things done.

In our context, *agile* is a broad church. Yes, it is primarily a mindset, but it's become an umbrella term for many other things. At the epicentre there's a core philosophy underpinning everything but there's much more besides, including ways of working – the how-to-do mechanics – such as the highly respected, widely used frameworks and a veritable smorgasbord of support ranging from cosy local groups to humungous international organisations.

Agile definitions

What is *agile*?

Agile is a label used in many different ways. In general usage it's used to describe the ability to move quickly and respond to change. But it's been adopted as a widely used tag for a new way of thinking and an innovative approach to getting things done.

Agile is a mindset and a way of life supported by well-established ways of working, values and principles, with a widespread, informal community of devoted followers.

We'll be looking closely at all the individual elements in the *agile* package. Put together, they provide everything needed to get better at what we do. It might be tempting to focus on one aspect, such as one of the frameworks, but reaping the full rewards requires looking at a full bundle: the thinking, the culture, the ways of working and support. Put together they're a powerful mix.

The *agile* modus operandi is centred on self-organising, cross-functional teams who deliver incrementally in handy-size chunks instead of trying to deliver it all in one go. Whatever the size of the team, it must have the capability to deliver whatever product or service the business needs without outside help. The first delivery is always the minimum required to get going and is added to from there.

The most important things here are: What does this all achieve? What are the outcomes? Quite rightly, people want to know what's in it for them if they go for it.

Go faster, be cheaper, get better

Agile is very much about delivering end product whatever form it takes. It can be a physical thing that can be held and admired or a service that can be used and appreciated. At the very heart of the matter is the desire to constantly deliver ever improving products or services in the shortest possible timeframe, and at a great price. Aiming to go faster, be cheaper and to constantly get better are central to the *agile* way.

Faster, cheaper and better is a mantra that's dogged *agile* in some respects, as it's considered by some to be an over-used soundbite about potential. But there's no doubt this is the ultimate target for any business and it's a specific, measurable aspiration that everyone can relate to. Time, cost and quality are the three forces that forge any endeavour and there's substance to claims about what *agile* can achieve.

Go faster

Time is a valuable resource and we all recognise the advantages of doing things as quickly as possible. *Go faster* comes in many guises but is especially evident in the initial time to market for your product or service. *Agile* focusses on getting the minimum needed for launch out pronto, with the added bells and whistles to be layered on top afterwards.

This doesn't compromise quality. It just means that at launch time the end product is fit-for-purpose and nothing more. No delays while those nice-to-have extras are added in and this speed-to-market can be more important than anything – it can be a deal maker or breaker. Look at the evolution of Apple products and Amazon services as examples of this in action.

Be cheaper

Cost is another important consideration, and sometimes it's even the primary driver. While there's no cast iron guarantee that the final bill will be cheaper with *agile,* by getting to market quicker it means the launch cost is considerably less – at times a fraction of the anticipated overall cost. This means any idea can be properly checked out and market-tested without breaking the bank.

After lift-off, products and services can evolve on a regular, piece-by-piece basis. Each additional delivery targets immediate customer needs and is at an inexpensive extra cost. This is not only a delight for customers, it's easy to get early feedback and allows for a low-cost change in direction whenever necessary.

Get better

Mistakes will happen, that's a fact of life. It's equally true that nothing's perfect and there's always scope for improvements. *Agile* culture embraces all of this and puts the spotlight on learning and improving. Much emphasis is put on keeping a watchful eye on things and continually striving to constantly get better by polishing the products, services and even the processes themselves.

This doesn't legitimise being slapdash and the intention is to get it right the first time whenever possible. But rather than insist on perfection up front, it's more effective to settle for *good enough* with honing to follow if needed. The *agile* culture is one where reflecting on what's happened and searching for enhancements is the *de facto* standard.

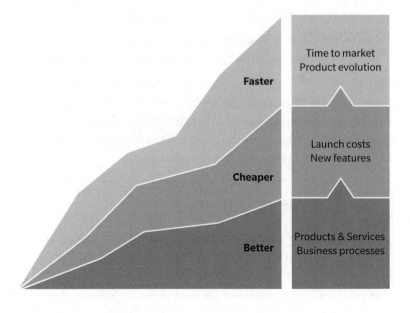

What's on offer?

Faster, cheaper and better is a great soundbite and we've dug into a few of the upshots that can be expected. But there's plenty more to tell the senior management team about if they want to see more flesh on the bone:

- **Quicker to market**: Delivering in bite-sized chunks shortens the time to market and produces a myriad of benefits, including early validation of the core idea.

- **Fit-for-purpose deliveries**: Continual business involvement ensures that the end product does exactly what it says on the tin.

- **Lower start-up costs**: The initial budget needed is much smaller and only winning ideas get additional investment. It's no longer necessary to bet the ranch on new ideas.

- **Change-friendly**: The ability to adjust and adapt is baked in and is even encouraged. It's never hampered by starting with a non-negotiable plan with no wiggle room.

- **Improved productivity**: Individual and team empowerment leads to a sense of ownership that improves productivity. There's no need to crack the whip to crank up output.

- **Learning culture**: Mistakes along the way are inevitable but now let's concentrate on learning from them and preventing repeats.

This all reduces risk and dramatically improves the likelihood of successful outcomes. Each one is a by-product of a standard implementation and you can expect to see results from day one. Finally, the good news is that everything needed to get started is right here in *Agile Now* – no additional ingredients required.

Go agile in 15 minutes

There's a high probability that the mantra of *faster, cheaper and better* appeals in principle but what will it mean in practice? Let's put flesh on the bones by looking back at your recent

---

endeavours and explore how *agile* might help. Fifteen minutes is all this will take.

It's a good idea to focus on one sizeable piece of work if possible. Preferably something close to home that you know the ins and outs about. It's even better if the outcome was important for whatever reason. Reflect on what happened in the context of the following questions:

- Were there any occasions when the time taken was too long? When the delay between having an initial bright idea and something useable being delivered seemed endless and there was a lost opportunity?

- When the final delivery arrived, was there a feeling of disappointment? Perhaps not quite what was expected or needed? Was there a shortfall of *must-have* core basic essentials? Were there too many unnecessary bells and whistles? Did it take much longer to deliver or cost more than anticipated?

- As work progressed was every clarification and minor adjustment touted as a change to the initial scope? Were penalties, extra costs or time delays threatened? Was every conversation about the devil in the detail held in a strained atmosphere?

Is any of this ringing a bell? Even one yes is enough. Agile offers a totally different way of thinking and operating where these problems will be a thing of the past. Read on to find out how.

Let this book be your guide

There's a mountain of material available about every aspect of *agile*. Books, articles, forums, and that's not to mention training courses, get-togethers and conferences. Spoilt for choice is the expression that springs to mind. But at the start of the journey, there can be too much information available and it can be difficult to see the wood for the trees. At times it's hard to know what's needed and it helps to have a simple guide pointing you in the right direction.

Agile Now is an intentionally quick read aimed to get you off to a fast start. It provides the essence of what's on offer, the foundation stones for getting the best results and guidance to avoid the major pitfalls. Whether you're a total novice or already on the road there's everything you need. And even world-weary veterans might appreciate going back to basics (especially if there's an interview looming in the near distance).

The two meatiest chapters in this book cover the how-to mechanics off-the-shelf frameworks for going *agile*. But in many respects the heart is to be found in the shorter chapters on developing the right mindset and the cultural angle of always looking for improvements. The final cherry on the top delves into the vast array of support and guidance available. All the chapters can stand alone but there's power in the union.

Each chapter is packed with practical advice and has exercises to help put ideas into practice. There are 'Go *agile* in 15 minutes' mini exercises and this should be taken literally as each one is something that can be done straight away. 'Go *agile* in an hour' sets an upper time limit and hopefully it can be slotted in sometime the same day. If you happen to have a bit of free time, then there's nothing to stop picking up any of these in isolation.

It helps to try before you buy, and even if it isn't the answer for you *Agile Now* will help you to work that out.

Go *agile* in 15 minutes

Drop me an email

If you're considering implementing *Agile,* or have started on that journey and need a helping hand, then drop me an email at: rob.cole@brilliantpm.co.uk with all the details. Always glad to help!

Start small, start fast

Reading this book cover-to-cover is a good first step but it's not the end of the story. The true measure of success is in putting these ideas into action – either as part of a bigger corporate rollout or by pushing the boat out personally. By the final chapter everything will be in place to do one or the other and there are several ways for this to happen.

You might get lucky and come in one day to hear the CEO (or suchlike) boldly announcing plans to go *agile*. But that's a rarity and in the vast majority of cases it's a slow burner with the fuse being lit with a pilot project of some sort. It doesn't matter too much about how big the first job is, the key is to have an early win and build from there. Success breeds success and once the ball starts rolling it's easier to win friends and influence people.

There may even be objections that are impossible to overcome, or little appetite for a formal pilot in the near future. The good news is that *agile* doesn't have to be launched with a huge fanfare and widespread senior management approval. There are options for a legitimate launch slightly below the radar and if all else fails then *personal agility* is the perfectly acceptable backstop. We'll look more closely at all these options later on.

Whatever the route in, the risks are minimal and the upside is potentially immense. The set-up costs are next to nothing in terms of hard cash and it is reasonable to expect results from day one. As we explore ideas and techniques, think about where they apply to you and your colleagues, the team you work with and the wider organisation. *Agile* is geared up to be easily applied and there's no substitute for giving it a go soon.

Agile won't float everyone's boat. In the same way that it isn't a natural fit for every task, project or organisational mission, then it applies with knobs on when it comes to individuals. But even if going gung-ho is a non-starter then there's plenty on offer than can be used in isolation. Some people use *agile* all of the time, but everyone can use it some of the time. There's something here for everyone.

See *agile* in action

It's much easier to tune into ideas when there's a working example to relate to. From time to time the ideas in this book will be applied to the development of a new business called AgileParcs, which will replicate the popular European camping park model. It's a start-up and there are plans to offer a mixture of accommodation, ranging from traditional camping to mobile homes. The intention is to start small and build from there.

A site has been acquired in an area in south-west England popular with holidaymakers. There's already a five-bedroom character house operating as a B&B and several acres of adjacent land available. Fortunately, there are no legal issues to worry about, the local bank has extended reasonable working capital and the locals love the idea. Of course, even *agile* can't guarantee those things normally.

The AgileParcs crew collectively decided to take an *agile* approach to the development. There's no truth in the rumour they're hoping to emulate the success of CentreParcs, but hey that would be lovely.

Agile in action

AgileParcs case study

The B&B business is reasonably successful but hampered by limited capacity – customers are regularly turned away, especially in the summer. Despite the pent-up demand, there are some concerns about whether there are enough potential punters for a sizeable camping site.

The management team at AgileParcs is risk-adverse and funds are limited. They don't want to get into too much debt and see this as potentially a ten-year project. The ideal end target is a medium-sized, high-quality holiday park with all the trimmings.

There are different opinions within the organisation about the optimum mix of accommodation. Everything from high-spec mobile homes, luxury lodges and comfortable pitches for those wanting to do the real thing are being considered.

For the initial launch opinions are being considered. Maybe an inexpensive start by marking off an area for tents and another for motorhomes. That's enough to begin trading and get the revenue following in.

Starting small and building from there certainly is appealing financially and it would make it easy to try out ideas and change direction if necessary.

An agile, incremental approach would ensure a fast start-up with plenty of opportunities for quick wins. Maybe no swimming pool on day one, but let's keep it in mind for the future. An ideal candidate for thinking agile.

The famous *Agile Manifesto*

Agile is a much broader church than most realise even if it appears that techies are leading the charge. This misunderstanding stems from a big push from the tech community at the start of the millennium when a passionate bunch of software developers met up in a ski resort and produced the *Manifesto for agile software development*. Perhaps quite not in the same league as the *US Declaration of Independence*, but it continues to be a much-quoted statement of intent.

Manifesto for agile software development

We are uncovering better ways of developing software by doing it and helping others do it. Through this work we have come to value:

Individuals and interactions *over processes and tools*

Working software *over comprehensive documentation*

Customer collaboration *over contract negotiation*

Responding to change *over following a plan*

That is, while there is value in the items on the right, we value the items on the left more.

© *Agile Manifesto* Copyright 2001: Kent Beck, Mike Beedle, Arie van Bennekum, Alistair Cockburn, Ward Cunningham, Martin Fowler, James Grenning, Jim Highsmith, Andrew Hunt, Ron Jeffries, Jon Kern, Brian Marick, Robert C. Martin, Steve Mellor, Ken Schwaber, Jeff Sutherland, Dave Thomas. This declaration may be freely copied in any form, but only in its entirety through this notice.

This declaration signalled the start of a wider adoption of *agile* principles, with the technology world leading the charge. As the title indicates, the manifesto was intentionally IT centric and the accompanying surge was very much in that space. The good news is the software development business embraced *agile* with an evangelical desire to spread the word and that's certainly borne fruit over recent years.

A universal *agile charter*

With a touch of fine-tuning we can declare our own generic *Agile charter* based on the *Manifesto for agile software development* and the 12 principles that accompany it. But our version has a wider, more universal appeal:

Individuals and relationships *over the tools of the trade*

Delivering useful stuff *over rules and regulations*

Customer partnerships *over contractual small print*

Responding to change *over being inflexible*

1 Our highest priority is to satisfy the customer through early and continuous delivery of valuable ~~software~~ stuff.

2 Welcome changing requirements, even late in development. *Agile* processes harness change for the customer's competitive advantage.

3 Deliver working ~~software~~ things frequently, from a couple of weeks to a couple of months, with a preference to the shorter timescale.

4 Businesspeople and ~~developers~~ the team must work together daily throughout the project.

5 Build projects around motivated individuals. Give them the environment and support they need and trust them to finish the job.

6 The most efficient and effective method of conveying information to and within a *~~development~~ team* is face-to-face conversation.

7 Working ~~software~~ stuff is the primary measure of progress.

8 *Agile* processes promote sustainable development. The sponsors, ~~developers,~~ builders and users should be able to maintain a constant pace indefinitely.

9   Continuous attention to ~~technical~~ product excellence and good design enhances agility.

10 Simplicity – the art of maximising the amount of work not done – is essential.

11 The best ~~architectures,~~ frameworks, requirements and designs emerge from self-organising teams.

12 At regular intervals, the team reflects on how to become more effective, then tunes and adjusts its behaviour accordingly.

Admittedly it does help a little bit if you're coming from a technology background, as that sector of the community is very mature, with masses of experience to draw on. But unlike the freemasons, everyone is actively encouraged to join the gang. The bottom line is the who-said-what-and-when is probably of limited interest. What does matter is that these days *agile* is for everyone.

Watch out – *agile* risks about!

Agile isn't a miracle cure and things can go wrong. As we'll see throughout the book, there are plenty of pitfalls to guard against, and the biggest risks are at the start. A haphazard launch can put a massive hole in the ship even before setting off. Get the foundations right and it's unlikely you'll end up on the rocks.

Beware the *agile* launch tripwires!

There are risks with any new enterprises and going *agile* is no different. During the early days it's particularly important to avoid any bear traps with the potential to inflict a serious wound. Be mindful of the following:

- **Being overly ambitious**: Rome wasn't built in a day and there's no need to attempt a revolution. Feel free to start small, win friends and build from there.

- **Bowing to initial resistance**: There's going to be unbelievers but don't give up at the first knock-back. Demonstrate ideas and techniques to win people over.

- **Launching with an inappropriate mission**: Let's not begin our journey by building a space shuttle. Plenty of more suitable opportunities are available if you look around.

- **The wrong types of people involved**: Certain characters are less likely to embrace *agile*, so be selective, especially early on. An open-minded, can-do attitude goes a long way.

- **Unrealistic expectations**: Don't be tempted to oversell the benefits. There will be tangible benefits from day one but set reasonable expectations. Don't promise an overnight revolution.

- **Assuming it's all so simple**: It's pretty easy to get to grips with the basics but for the best results it's important to get behind the headlines.

Even with solid foundations, it's easy to make mistakes along the way. In fact, that's inevitable. Slip-ups aren't feared, the aim is they're not repeated. *Agile* comes well-equipped with built-in safety checks to ensure learning from experience is part of the lifestyle. This is the final piece of a golden triangle: the how-to mechanics, the right mindset and continuous improvements.

The final word

No organisation or individual is perfect and it's not a sensible option to stand still. The commercial success stories of recent years maintain their dominant positions by continually innovating and improving. The folks at Apple, Google and Amazon don't rest on their laurels and are always seeking to do things a little bit better. Their changes range from minor tweaks to massive leaps but the desire to move forward is central to everything they do.

Agile provides a total package for looking at what you're doing and helping to do it more effectively. *Quicker, cheaper and better,* as the well-known strapline goes. This includes anything from improving normal day-to-day routines right through to launching new initiatives. It also delivers a structure for risk-free innovation – everything from a way of thinking right through to practical advice.

Despite excellent press, the honeymoon period is drawing to a close and there are beginning to be rumblings of discontent. It's true to say that *agile* isn't a miracle cure and it does require a deft touch at times in order to live up to expectations. Fortunately, there are some excellent frameworks available to help keep things on track and all sorts of other support available once you know where to look – and *Agile Now* will be your guide.

Go *agile* in an hour

Identify what you need

Think about your current situation and what things need addressing. Nobody lives in a perfect world and sometimes a small tweak here or there makes all the difference. Sometimes, of course, the problems are deeper rooted and more fundamental. As you'll see, *agile* can help out wherever you are.

Think about the organisation you belong to, the team you're a part of, and your own needs. Reflect on how you spend 9 to 5 and the key challenges and blockers you face. Build up a wish list of things that would make your world a much better place.

Get your thoughts down somewhere so you can take a look back once you've read the book. By then, if all things go to plan, it will be clear how *agile* can chip in. There are a few blank pages immediately following this chapter specially for notes. Give each note a quick rating out of 5, where 1 is low importance to you and 5 is high.

Try to keep all this at the back of your mind when reading this book. Even take a quick look back at the end of finishing each chapter. Feel free to add things as you go along. The ultimate litmus test is whether *agile* can help.

At the very least, this reflection will be a nice health check of the way things are currently done. Hopefully, we'll achieve a hell of a lot more.

chapter 2

Work faster and better with *agile*

"If you don't know where you're going, you'll end up someplace else."

Yogi Berra

A sneak preview of Chapter 2

At the heart of *agile* is an innovative approach to managing your workload, the mechanics for operating more effectively:

- **Define the end in mind**: Be clear about where you're going to avoid getting side-tracked or lost.
- **Set out the stall**: Visualise the bite-size chunks needed to deliver your dream.
- **Choose what's most important**: Separate the essential must-haves from the bells and whistles.
- **Pin down the starter pack**: Work out the bare minimum set of features needed for launch.

Brighter days ahead

Working our socks off is admirable but it counts for nowt if we're side-tracked into doing things for no clear rhyme or reason – especially poorly thought out projects or management whims with dubious business value. Sadly, this happens too often and it's not only a waste of effort, it's a lost opportunity to make better use of our precious time. How mad and maddening is that?

What we do and how we do it is centre stage with *agile*. It provides a comprehensive, end-to-end framework for managing our work and makes sure we've thought about where we want to get to – which stops us from wandering aimlessly. Then once we've set out our stall, it guides and drives us through the nitty gritty with our target firmly in mind. It's all about delivering end results. Stuff that's fit-for-purpose, delivered on time and at a fair price.

Agile guides us into doing the right things and in a sensible order. Quite a heady cocktail that adds up to working smarter without having to graft any harder. Getting more out of limited resources and achieving far better outcomes. It provides a highly effective framework for defining and managing work and, as you'll see, it's blissfully easy to get started.

Know where you're going

Starting any new piece of work can be daunting, and it is surprising how many journeys begin without a clear end destination in mind. It can happen with an individual focused on a specific task, a team working on a big project or even when the Board of Directors is pinning down their corporate five-year plan. Sleeves get rolled up and people crack on before there's an end in mind and a final destination to work towards.

All *agile* endeavours are geared towards an end goal and this is referred to as either the *Vision* or the *Product Vision*. The *Vision* statement is an elevator pitch, a snappy summary of what the product is all about. Don't get this mixed up with a traditional

Mission Statement which can be cliché-ridden and detached from the real graft going on in the organisation. A *Product Vision* is never vague or ambiguous.

The end goal is rarely achieved in one single leap. Normally it comes about in a series of smallish steps. Effort along the way must keep us moving in the right direction and that will be a primary measure of our success and of business worth. It's like in a chess game where every move is another step towards checkmate, even when it's necessary to take a sideways step before moving on again.

It always makes sense to start from a clear idea of what you want to achieve. It might be argued it's just common sense. It's a recurring theme that *agile* draws heavily on sound judgement, and that is certainly the case here.

What, why and who's it for

The first step is to pin down what you're trying to achieve in a way that's easy to communicate and validate progress against. Get the ball rolling by identifying *What's Wanted*, *Who's It for* and *Why Is It*

Needed. It's important to resist the temptation to just get on with doing stuff without first thinking about what, who for and why. The end result should be pithy and strike a chord with everyone involved in the work and your target customers.

- **What is needed?**: It can be an end product or a consumable service, but it needs to be specific and measurable. It can't be a series of activities like discussions or meetings. If this can't be articulated, then alarm bells are ringing.

- **Who is the customer in mind?**: Whether it's a commissioned job for an individual punter or a launch into a new market, there will be someone in mind. If not, it's most probably a vanity project or a management whim.

- **Why is this needed?**: Either it solves a specific problem or there's some other compelling way the customer will benefit. It doesn't matter whether the target market is niche or if the appeal is wider, the same applies.

These might seem like simple questions, but far too often the temptation is to plough on with *real work* without pausing for thought. In a study of more than a hundred start-ups, a venture capital organisation found that the number one cause of failure was that there was no real market need. Close to half spent years building a product that no one was interested in.

This is another running theme of *agile* – check the obvious stuff that too often gets overlooked. The end result removes any doubt about *what, who* and *why* even to a casual observer.

Agile in action

A *Product Vision* for AgileParcs

To offer a variety of holiday accommodation for couples and families to choose from. To include tent pitches, mobile homes and lodges, providing the highest possible standards and facilities for their type, unlike other nearby holiday parks that are primarily price-focussed. The aim is to offer holiday lodgings of consistently high quality even if it costs a little bit more.

This may be nowhere near perfect but it's certainly fit-for-purpose. It's jargon-free and will strike a chord with everyone involved.

The AgileParcs *Product Vision* provides a wealth of information about what's going to be on offer, the potential customers and what will set it apart from the local competition. The end game is set out, including a pivotal declaration that high standards are vitally important and the reasons why. The big picture is there for the internal business team, investors and potential customers too. Plenty for everyone to hang their hat on.

Within the fixed end point there's plenty of room to manoeuvre regarding the detail of what will be delivered. Based on the *Vision*, it will be easy to pin down individual pieces of work and to measure progress towards the end goal. A bit of effort up front sets up a solid foundation for everything that follows and will, without doubt, pay back the time investment in spades.

Go agile in 15 minutes

Create a *Product Vision*

Look back on something recent that's close to your heart. It doesn't have to be a multi-million work project and a personal venture is fine, such as home improvement or the next family holiday. What was wanted, who was it for and why was it needed?

If it's easy to pin down the *Product Vision* and it was a successful mission, that says plenty. Probably the end game was in mind even if it wasn't set out up front. If it was a bit of a disaster, can the what, who and why be pinned down? A blurred *Vision* isn't usually the only reason for failure, but it can be a significant contributor.

> Now think about the *Vision* for an upcoming task or project, especially anything perceived as important or critical. If all's well it will be easy to articulate the *Vision* – merely a case of putting it into words.
>
> *If there's any head-scratching, you might be heading off on a fool's errand.*

Set out the stall

Any undertaking of consequence involves more than just one simple task and is typically made up of numerous discrete steps. Whether this is executed by one person or by a gang, it adds up to what's commonly called a project (*an individual or collaborative team effort that's carefully planned to achieve a particular aim*). In the simplest sense, a project is a set of connected pieces of work. We all work on projects of some sort from time to time.

An *agile* project is defined by the *Product Vision* and can be broken down into a series of moves towards the end destination, with each one delivering its own specific business value. Every step is plainly described in business-speak, not technical jargon, in a way that those interested can relate to. The expected outcomes, the stuff to be delivered in each case, is clearly specified and is the primary measure of a job well done.

Once lumped together, this collection of linked steps is widely known in *agile* circles as the *Backlog*. More jargon. Without wanting to get bogged down by terminology, it certainly helps to know a few key terms, and this is one that will constantly crop up. It is sometimes pointed out that it's nothing more than a sophisticated to-do list. Quite right, and all the better for being easy to explain and understand.

When the *Backlog* is first created, don't overthink things. It's an opportunity for the business team to brainstorm their hopes and dreams, to get everything down on paper for further reflection.

It's perfectly fine for the first pass to be a stepping stone, a collection that moves things in the right direction strategically, pinning down all and everything necessary from the off.

Agile in action
Drafting the *Backlog* for AgileParcs

Tents, mobile homes and lodges were obvious options. During the AgileParcs *Backlog* brainstorming, it was agreed to offer luxury glamping as a unique selling point. Tree houses, pods, bell tents, yurts, shepherd's huts and even a converted London bus were suggested.

Shower blocks, toilets and a reception-cum-admin building were also proposed. A kiddies playground, indoor and outdoor swimming pools and even an entertainment centre was mentioned. And a couple of less exciting but essential items were identified: areas for ordinary waste bins and recycling facilities.

Draft *Backlog* items:

- Tent pitches
- Mobile homes
- Caravans
- Wooden lodges
- Yurts
- Shower/toilet blocks
- Reception/admin building
- Entertainment centre/bar
- Swimming pool
- Communal hot tub
- Waste bins
- Recycling facilities
- Entrance sign

> Plenty of must-haves plus a few bells and whistles. Each item is specific and delivers business value in its own right, and yet it's easy to see there'll be plenty of room to manoeuvre along the way.
>
> *This is all very much in line with the AgileParcs Product Vision.*

There'll be occasions when a comprehensive *Backlog* can be pinned down up front. But this is very rare and more often the first stab only gets us travelling in the right direction, especially with big endeavours. One of the selling points of *agile* is that it's not necessary to pin down absolutely everything before setting off. Ensure that the essential requirements are identified – the core nucleus of the *Vision* – and throw in some nice-to-have luxuries for consideration too.

Things are bound to be missed; don't lose sleep about that either. It's not normal to be able to think of everything up front. There's an expectation that items will be added in and that the *Backlog* is not etched in stone, but on the contrary is constantly evolving. *Agile* is especially strong when it comes to changing your mind and it's easy-peasy to make tweaks and adjustments. Change is embraced, not frowned upon.

Once the initial wish list is identified, the next step is for each individual slice of work to be written up as a business requirement like a job card – drilling down further into the detail of what exactly is wanted, who it will appeal to and why it will appeal. This is widely referred to as a *User Story*, another piece of much-used jargon. Not the most descriptive tag but easy enough to understand and remember.

Agile in action

Creating an AgileParcs *User Story*

Creating a space to put up a tent, known as a tent pitch, is a small piece of work with a specific deliverable and with value to the business. In this case a spot that can be rented and used by a camping customer.

There are practical considerations to consider: one tent pitch in isolation makes limited sense from both the construction and sales perspectives. Also, the vast majority of customers will want enough room to park their car alongside. All that can be specified, and the *User Story* was drafted as follows.

10 co-located tent pitches

As a sales consultant at AgileParcs, I want a strip of flat, grassy ground so that I can offer simple, low-cost accommodation for up to 10 tent owners. Each tent space must be big enough for a large family tent with room for a car nearby. The block of pitches must be within a short walk of the shower/toilet block.

When it was reviewed by the team it was observed that *User Stories* are best written up from the end customer's perspective. In this case it would be along the lines of "As a customer AgileParcs, I want a strip of flat, grassy ground for my family tent with space for our car next to it." The team added that ten co-located pitches should be factored in as the initial, minimum requirement.

There are many ways to skin a cat.

Each *User Story* must have a specific outcome that delivers business value and builds towards the *Product Vision*. If there are any other considerations, they can be specified too. Get down all the known requirements and constraints without going in detail about how the work will be carried out.

Put it all on show

Openness is a pillar of *agile* and all forms of transparency are vigorously encouraged. There's plenty of upside to keeping everyone in the loop and with that in mind, choosing where to keep our *Backlog* of *User Stories* is an important consideration. Writing everything in a notebook and locking it away in a secure drawer isn't in the right spirit. Far better to have everything on display, the higher the profile the better.

Loading *User Stories* on to a physical wallboard in a central location is a very popular option. It serves as a hub and an information radiator. Expect curious interest and encourage feedback. The wider the engagement, the greater the validation of intentions, with the possible added bonus of new ideas being generated. A wallboard is an invaluable way of promoting interest and feedback. Last but certainly not least, there's no better way of advertising intentions.

Go *agile* in 15 minutes

Create a DIY wallboard

Get hold of three blank sheets of A4 paper and stick them side by side in portrait mode on a nearby wall. Write 'TO DO' boldly at the top of the first one, ditto with 'IN PROGRESS' and 'DONE' at the top of the second and third.

Alternatively, you can use a flipchart as they're the perfect size (but pretty hard to find these days). Whiteboards are another popular variation. Or improvise, it really doesn't matter as long as it's a practical size and easy to put on prominent display.

Get a pack of Post-It notes, or something similar, and write out the most important things to do. Put a brief summary description at the top of each note with an explanatory sentence

---

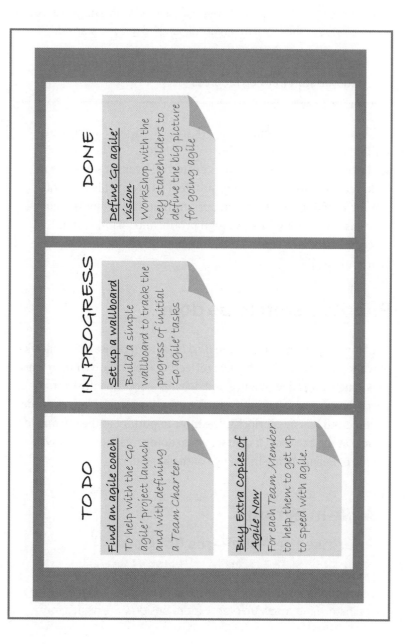

TO DO

Find an agile coach
To help with the 'Go agile' project launch and with defining a Team Charter

Buy Extra Copies of Agile Now
For each Team Member to help them to get up to speed with agile.

IN PROGRESS

Set up a wallboard
Build a simple wallboard to track the progress of initial 'Go agile' tasks

DONE

Define 'Go agile' vision
Workshop with the key stakeholders to define the big picture for going agile

underneath if necessary. No need to go mad with a huge list but try at least to think of a meaningful batch to get you started.

Hey presto, a high profile agile task board loaded up and ready to start tracking progress.

It's increasingly popular to work from home and a physical wallboard isn't practical in those circumstances. The same applies when the project team is dotted all over for some damn good reason. This isn't a major problem as *agile* is blessed with a number of digital task board options that make remote sharing very easy. They may lack the high profile and visibility of a physical board in a central location, but they do everything else brilliantly well.

Prioritise stuff to be done

The final step in assembling the *Backlog* is to organise these chunks of work into a sensible sequence reflecting their relative importance. This is never an exact science and debates – occasionally heated – are part of the process. Begin by shuffling the *User Stories* into the order of perceived business priority, the most important at the top and least critical at the bottom. Of course, when doing this there's always a degree of beauty being in the eye of the beholder.

Agile in action
Prioritise the AgileParcs *Backlog*

Underpinning the *Vision* for AgileParcs is a variety of different accommodation options for prospective punters, and the *Backlog* brainstorming threw up plenty more besides. So, what's the best pecking order? There are some obvious relative priorities, but on the whole it's not a straightforward call.

There's an argument in favour of starting with low-cost, low-risk tent pitches. Or perhaps beginning with high-revenue mobile homes and lodges, then slotting in the relatively low-income tent site at the very end? The only certain thing is a swimming pool is a low priority unless it's an inflatable one.

Looking at useful but non-essential items, things will function more smoothly with proper check-in and check-out facilities. A small convenience shop stocked with essentials will be much appreciated especially if there's also information on activities to do and places to visit in the surrounding area. The optimum sequence of delivery is a matter of judgement and here's the first draft:

- Tent pitches
- Waste bins
- Shower/toilet block
- Recycling facilities
- Yurts
- Entrance sign
- Reception/admin building/shop
- Wooden lodges
- Mobile homes
- Caravans
- Entertainment centre/bar
- Communal hot tub
- Swimming pool

Prioritising is certainly not an exact science. So, like the AgileParcs team, get the Backlog into a reasonable running order and then fine-tune.

Although there's never a right answer when it comes to putting things in an order of importance, it's prudent to be able to walk before trying to run. So, a good variety of accommodation plus a check-in facility is always going to be higher up the wish list than a communal hot tub. There's no need to fret about getting the priorities spot on up front because the running order can be easily changed, with items promoted or demoted when necessary.

The AgileParks *Backlog* is a living thing and it's a healthy sign if stories are added and priorities change. Early on, the management team may realise it's impossible to operate without an office and a small temporary portacabin becomes a new requirement with a higher priority. Or customer surveys may indicate cosy lodges will be much more popular than anticipated and that gets moved up the pecking order too.

Sizing is important

An important think-piece when assessing relative priorities is the comparative size of each piece of work. When a job that delivers high value is up against one with little return then the decision is an easy one, but life is rarely that simple. Usually it's a choice between something with higher net worth that will cost more versus a quicker win that's less useful but cheaper to deliver.

This can be a minefield and tangible costs are usually the main things considered – basically any hard cash involved and number of hours of graft required. Predicting the fixed costs and anticipating the number of person hours to deliver certainly helps in deciding what to do first. However, there's a tendency to get bogged down in the calculations. This approach is time-consuming and the costs are only indicative anyway.

Agile estimation uses a different approach. Rather than chase the impossible goal of predicting exact costs, the aim is to get an indication of the relative size of work within the *Backlog*. Is *User Story* X bigger than Y? Is Y larger or smaller than Z and the size of each is described in a non-financial way. A very popular way of doing this is by assigning T-shirt sizes: XS, S, M, L, XL, XXL and even XXXL if you wish!

Crucially, with *agile,* estimates are always produced by the people who'll be doing the work. Elements considered do not include the potential effort required but also the complexity of the story and the number of unknown factors surrounding it.

Agile in action
AgileParcs size estimates

Is the tent pitch job bigger than the one for building the wooden lodge? Where does the admin block/convenience store fit into the scale? And what about those new-fangled yurts? The important thing is to define the relative size of planned work in the *Backlog,* as follows:

- Tent pitches – S
- Waste bins – XS
- Shower/toilet block – XXL
- Recycling facilities – XS
- Yurts – M
- Entrance signage – XS
- Reception/admin building/shop – XL
- Wooden lodges – XL
- Mobile homes – L
- Caravans – L
- Entertainment centre/bar – XXXL
- Communal hot tub – M
- Swimming pool – XXL

Don't be surprised if you don't agree with these initial estimates. The sizing exercise always sparks valuable debate.

When there are differences of opinion it usually points to misunderstandings about exactly what is involved or highlights unknown factors. Is it best for AgileParcs to deliver the caravans, mobile homes and wooden lodges one at a time or in batches of two or three? Are the lodges going to be handcrafted from scratch or shipped in as a package and then assembled? If the admin block is bigger, can it incorporate a convenience store, general storage and even a coffee shop or bar?

The generalness of the T-shirt assessments avoids prolonged debate about minor points of detail. Once *User Stories* are identified as S, M, L or whatever, then this assessment is a useful factor in juggling priorities. Business value is the primary driver but there are occasions when an XXXL valuation may tip the balance in favour of other low-hanging fruit.

Go *agile* in 15 minutes

Build a prioritised *Backlog*

After grabbing a coffee, quickly brainstorm a list of the things you need to do today. Don't agonise, get everything down – even the nice-to-haves-if-time-permits. Check that every task produces something explicit that will be of use in its own right.

Put your to-do list into running order and let gut feel be your guide. Then tag each item with a T-shirt size of S, M, L or XL and have another think in case there are any quick wins which deserve pushing up the pecking order, or complex tasks that are candidates for demotion.

Think about what you absolutely must do before going home and check it's an achievable target. If it is, then you've pinned down the minimum you need to deliver before heading off with a clear conscience, and with plenty more to do if time permits.

Voilà, a prioritised Backlog.

Deliver in bite-size chunks

Before *agile* came along, the most popular approach to project planning was to spend ages detailing a huge long list of requirements and then insist they're all essential from day one. This included endless deliberation about all the bells, whistles and other nice-to-haves which could take months or even years in extreme cases. Many great ideas died a slow and painful death this way even before any real work started.

Of course, everything isn't really needed up front. But in the bad old days, anyone with any nous knew that the first delivery was probably all you'll get apart from fixes to any glaring snags. There was little point in hoping for anything that wasn't very clearly specified in the contract signed up front. To make matters worse, there was a long, long, long wait for anything to turn up and hell to pay if any changes were asked for along the way.

In stark contrast, *agile* delivers smaller chunks regularly. Starting with the most important stuff first and then working through the wish list, with plenty of opportunity to change track when necessary. A constant stream of smaller deliveries with plenty of scope for a rethink whenever needed. This is referred to as *Incremental Delivery*, with each bundle building on the previous one.

Agile definitions

Definition of Done

The AgileParcs *Vision* sets up the big picture but it isn't enough to judge when each individual task is complete. As a general rule of thumb, for any job to be considered done at the end of the workflow, the end product must be fit-for-purpose and ready to go. There were different opinions about what that meant in practice.

The AgileParcs team drafted a *Definition of Done* which applies to all their work. It included a series of conditions to keep the design team, construction, sales and marketing, internal maintenance and finance teams happy. Of course, the main focus was on the hard graft, but all the touches needed to make it a saleable commodity were there too.

All sorts of boring wrap-up activities and admin were included as well. The site must be cleared, tools and equipment tidied away, timesheets filled in and handed over to the finance department. Plus, they added on a lighter note, a celebratory cup of tea and a bit of cake for the workers in the staff canteen.

The Definition of Done spells out without ambiguity how to confirm each task is complete. There's no set format and it's always a collaborative effort.

Build a foundation

The first no-frills package that goes out is the foundation stone of the *Vision* and is known as the *Minimum Viable Product,* usually abbreviated to *MVP.* The jargon is a bit mind-boggling but the underlying concept is simple enough: it's the bare essentials needed to get going, with the intention to kick on from there. Using this approach, it's cheaper to get started and easier to change direction if things don't pan out quite as expected.

The tricky question is what's the minimum needed to get started. Defining the *MVP* isn't always plain sailing and is often a hot potato. Of course, the smaller the *MVP,* the earlier the first usable chunk arrives. But it must be fully functional too and it must be viable as a standalone product or service. It's certainly fine for AgileParcs to start with only tent pitches and mobile homes but there would be no point in launching with an admin block but no accommodation.

Agile definitions
The *Minimum Viable Product*

The majority of *agile* terminology slips off the tongue and is close to self-explanatory. One big exception to the rule is *Minimum Viable Product* (*MVP*) which is both a mouthful and often misrepresented. In an attempt to avoid overcomplicating this concept, let's say the common usage is *just enough core features to be useful.*

Developing a complex product or a service takes time and is costly. Far better to launch with the bare minimum needed and see if it hits the mark. This way, the time to market is considerably reduced and it's easy to see if things are on the right track. If they are, additional features can be added over time and if not, it's easy to change course.

Getting the balance right between too much and too little is one of the biggest challenges. It's important to be ruthless in identifying the *MVP* without going overboard. Pulling any item out should have severe consequences and effectively prevent the ship from setting sail. Anything with an acceptable temporary workaround shouldn't be included initially.

There's likely to be a sharp intake of breath once this is pinned down. There's scope for manoeuvre but always ask whether it's best to get the must-haves out quickly or to wait longer for a more wide-ranging offering.

With a fully functioning physical or digital task board in place, it's much easier to stand back and reflect on the minimum requirements. It easy to shuffle around the *User Stories* and discuss permutations with others. When doing this, always bear in mind that once the *MVP* is launched, other stuff will be coming soon afterwards. Normally it's better to keep the *MVP* slimline and accept some short-term pain to get off to a fast start.

Beware the *agile* workflow tripwires!

There are risks with any new endeavour and when things go badly wrong it usually starts to unravel right at the start. It's important to set up a solid foundation to avoid going off piste early on. Be mindful of the following:

- **Lack of *Vision***: It's easy to underestimate the importance of defining what, who and why. It's time well spent and if it's not a straightforward exercise then the alarm bells are ringing.

- **An ill-formed *Backlog*:** It's easy to go through the motions and look the part, but a fully functioning *Backlog* is the ultimate indicator of *agile* health.

- **Understated *Minimum Viable Product*:** The *MVP* must be a useable and connected set of features that's of value to the end customer. At least the minimum needed to get started.

- **Neglected, static *Backlog*:** Setting up the *Backlog* and defining the *MVP* is only the start – it must be alive and moving at all times. A stale one means trouble.

Getting the Backlog into good shape is a flying start. It provides the healthy backbone needed for everything agile.

The final word

Managing work is a massive challenge and too often people just muddle through. Doing the right things and in the optimum order might sound like child's play but is never easy in practice. *Agile* provides a comprehensive approach to handling the workflow that's easy to grasp and implement. It's an end-to-end framework for getting off to a fast start and delivering regularly from there.

The *agile* piece-by-piece approach revolutionises the relationship between the doers and the receivers. No more waiting for *The twelfth of never* as it provides regular, concrete evidence that things are on the right track – far more reassuring than any project status report. In fact, it's a sign of things working well when the business starts to complain because they must wait *weeks* for what they want.

This brave new world does have its own special terminology and it helps to learn a bit of *agile*-speak. A handful of words and phrases are enough and already we're comfortable with shaping our *Product Vision*, writing up our *User Stories* and adding them to the *Backlog*. We're even thinking about what's in our *Minimum Viable Product* and looking forward to the *Incremental Delivery* of the rest.

Go *agile* in an hour

Start small, start now

At the heart of *agile* there's a revolutionary way for managing your workload and there's nothing wrong with diving straight in. Pick on a small piece of work that's needed soon, then *go for it*. Anything from a couple of days to a week is ideal. Don't go overboard and be wary of anything high profile or strategic.

- **Pin down the end game**: Spell out *what* is going to be on offer, *who* the target customers are and *why* this is a compelling proposition. It needs to be tangible enough to predict the key steps needed along the way and to guide decisions. If there are knowing nods from the people footing the bill, it means you're off to a flying start.

- **Break out the main tasks**: Work out the steps needed to reach the final destination. Define a series of moves to deliver the hopes and dreams of the business. Each must deliver something specific that's immediately useable and with standalone business value.

- **Build a running order**: Start by putting them in order of perceived worth. Then consider adjustments if there are any quick wins or smart short-term tactical moves. The to-do list must contain the essential components of the *Vision* and hopefully a bit more, all in a sensible sequence.

- **Ring-fence the minimum needed to launch**: Strip out all the nice-to-haves and identify the absolute minimum needed to get started. The smaller this first package is, the earlier the first usable delivery arrives, but remember it must be fully functional. Temporary workarounds and short-term pain are acceptable but get the balance right between time to market and usability.

- **Get it out there**: Find an in-your-face location for a physical wallboard or set up a shared digital version and then load up the work to be done. Keep it simple, with just three columns to begin with: TO DO, IN PROGRESS and DONE. The more high profile and accessible the better, as there's no better way of advertising *agile* intentions and demonstrating progress.

  You're off! The board can now be used to track work in progress and identify things that are done and dusted. Once set up, there's only a minimal overhead to keeping it going and you get to use agile in a real, live scenario.

chapter 3

Use agile to keep improving

"Even perfection has room for improvement."

Ty Warner

A sneak preview of Chapter 3

Agile constantly puts the spotlight on learning from experience and continuous improvement, getting benefits from the good, the bad and the ugly.

- **Look back and learn**: What do you do well? What can you do better? How to learn from *all* experience.
- **Check the production line**: See how to analyse the current ways of working and tease out improvements.
- **Get to the root cause**: Discover how to deal with underlying issues instead of the symptoms.
- **Constantly improve as a way of life**: Techniques to help build learning into the daily regime.

In search of a better world

Standing still in life, commonly referred to as resting on your laurels, is a dangerous option – this applies to both organisations and individuals. The corporate graveyard, in particular, provides plenty of examples of what can happen when there's an inability to adapt and improve – companies snuffed out and people surplus to requirements.

There's always room to do better. It's only a question of how much scope there is. There are occasions when improvement opportunities are pretty obvious and others when it requires a moment of pure genius to come up with a winning idea. Even fine-tuning can make a big difference, especially a series of small tweaks over a long period of time. If there's any doubt about all of this, then look no further than Apple as a prime example.

Searching for improvements is a central part of the *agile* way of life. The underlying philosophy is to be constantly on the lookout for ways to get better at what we do. This search is in no way meant as implied criticism. There's no suggestion intended that things aren't well and there's a need for people to pull their socks up. Part of the challenge is creating an environment where constantly searching for improvements is the norm.

This builds on the *agile* framework for defining and managing work, with the capability of taking it to even greater heights. Once again, as you'll see, there's no rocket science involved, and the process can begin straightaway.

Begin right now

One of the founding principles of *agile* is to continually *inspect and adapt* – and the perfect way to look for improvements is to ask the people already doing the work. There's no need to get in consultants or an independent time and motion expert to find out what can be done better. Without doubt, the existing gang will have plenty of ideas if they're asked.

Look to engage the members of the team you're in or a collection of close individuals with similar interests. As long as they have something tangible in common, give it a go. For maximum effect, it must be done collaboratively in a mini-workshop, not via a series of individual interviews. An hour is enough to get the ball rolling.

Only two very simple yet fundamental questions are needed: What do we do well? And what can we do better? The aim is to identify generic lessons that can be acted on, preferably immediately. Concentrate on positive recommendations that anyone can act on and avoid finger pointing even when blatant bad practice is the spark. This is not about getting people together to pinpoint blame or to pursue personal vendettas.

It's important to keep a watchful eye on any negative elements, especially in the first ever session. It can smooth proceedings to start with a round of positive points (what went well), before diving into those things that didn't go so brilliantly. Admittedly, there's usually a tendency for people to find it easier to look back and be critical but don't let that set an unconstructive tone.

The idea of learning lessons from experience isn't new but is usually seen as an optional nice-to-have. *Agile* however attaches great importance to this as a regular event and this type of reflective gathering is widely known as a *Retrospective*. It can be used at anytime and anywhere.

Go *agile* in 15 minutes

A mini personal *Retrospective*

An *agile Retrospective* is one of the best-known set pieces in town and at the heart of each session are two very basic questions: What do we do well? What can we do better? The spotlight is on what can be learned from past experience with a focus on actions to promote good practice and prevent the re-occurrence of bad stuff.

> This is usually a big set piece involving all the key players in a team or working together on a venture. But there's plenty of value in asking yourself those same questions in a standalone, personal *Retrospective*. It can be treated as an isolated exercise or used as preparation for the main event. Very useful either way.
>
> *As with the main event, stay firmly focussed on generating generic recommendations that can be implemented in the future. This is not a whodunnit or a witch hunt.*

One of the biggest risks is in generating too many recommendations and not being able to see the wood for the trees. Less is more, especially with early *Retrospectives*. A handful of highly effective actions is far better than reams of half-baked ideas. If each of the participants ends up with a follow-up action, that's perfect. And a fine indicator of success is when there are comments like "We should have done this yonks ago".

Get to the root cause

Getting folk together and extracting the maximum out of their collective experiences can pay big dividends. But be careful to identify what's at the heart of the points raised and pinpoint the root cause of everything good, bad and ugly. Don't get hung up with the symptoms. It's also important to distinguish between simple issues with obvious solutions and more complex matters that need looking into more closely.

Think like a doctor. When you visit the local GP most of the time the diagnosis is straightforward. Maybe an appointment at the fracture clinic, a course of antibiotics or even a verdict of nothing to worry about as it's a bug that's going around. But there are times when there's a symptom that needs more investigation as a precaution or a complex issue that requires much more thinking about.

The same applies to analysing observations made during *Retrospectives*. Don't be suckered into assuming an issue that is simple to describe has a no-brainer solution. A sixth sense for when there might be deeper roots will build up over time but until then be inquisitive about the underlying cause of everything noted, especially anything with a big impact.

Agile in action
AgileParcs *Retrospectives*

As AgileParcs is in essence a start-up, the learning opportunities were there early on and it was initially agreed to hold monthly *Retrospectives*. At times these were lengthy affairs and after a few months the team agreed to hold them fortnightly with a hard cap on the maximum duration of 90 minutes.

The core format stuck with what went well or could be done better as the starting prompts, but the team found it useful to limit each person to three observations to reduce the risk of overrunning. They found this restriction encouraged everyone to focus in on their top priorities.

For anything that went pear-shaped and was considered high impact, the team use the *5 Whys* technique to tease out the underpinning issue. Asking why it went wrong, then using the answer as the basis of the next question and so on. Up to five whys but usually two or three is more than enough.

AgileParcs is an ideal breeding ground for valuable lessons. It's an ambitious project with plenty of opportunities for going off piste, making outright gaffes and having moments of pure inspiration.

Don't forget to follow up

It's important that people feel they are being heard, and it can be therapeutic to let off steam from time to time. But it's even more important that the contributors see their feedback is taken seriously and acted on. Even when a treasure trove of material is generated, success or failure depends on what happens immediately after the main event. So, get cracking on the actions and get the ball rolling within days.

It's equally important that *Retrospectives* aren't one-offs or happen once in a blue moon. Build on the momentum from the first session by booking regular slots. If your team is enthusiastic then keep it snappy at 45 minutes or an hour max. If the team opt for monthly or more, then never miss a session, even at Christmas when the eggnog is flowing.

Continuous improvement is the lifeblood of *agile*. It keeps the processes alive and fresh by tapping into the hands-on experience of the people who know best. Get into the habit of treating learning lessons as an essential must-have and don't fall into the trap of treating them as a negotiable nice-to-have.

Check your production line

Retrospectives are a rich source for improvements, but the focus is very much on recent activities. An excellent add-on to this is to widen the net and take a closer look at the production line in its entirety. To scrutinise how stuff is produced from end-to-end and see if there are any problem areas and bottlenecks.

This is what Toyota pioneered under the *Lean* umbrella in the 1950s. Producing high-quality cars remained its top priority but it ingrained into daily life a desire to improve its vehicles, to shave delivery times and to reduce costs. *Lean* at Toyota is seen as the forerunner of the modern movement and is referred to in revered tones for the trailblazing search to reduce waste.

It lit the blue touch paper for the *agile* movement, partly because *Lean* techniques are so easy to replicate in any organisation. Admittedly, your workflows may not be as clearly defined and regimented as an assembly line for cars but there's always an element of repetitive cookie-cutting in what we do – typically starting at A and ending up at Z with pre-defined steps along the way.

Maybe a few slight variations, yet always a hard core of repeated processes.

Don't be overawed at the prospect of following in the footsteps of Toyota. There's absolutely no need to pin down everything in one fell swoop. Review something pivotal to what you do that is known for being a *bit problematic at times*. Get all the key players involved in the evaluation and begin with a simple overview of the end-to-end steps – the flow of work. Include who-does-what and any important decisions along the way.

A written, descriptive narrative works reasonably well but the best bang for buck is one of the many variations of *Process Map Diagrams* that visually show the work activities and the people involved. Mapping a process is done by simply drawing a box for each step and connecting them with arrows to show the flow.

Less is more with this. Keep it simple and keep it high level as it's extremely important to be able to see the wood for the trees. It's perfectly adequate to use a whiteboard, a selection of coloured pens and plenty of common sense.

Agile in action

AgileParcs business process mapping

Flush with success from their *Retrospective* sessions, the AgileParcs team decided to go for an end-to-end review of their most pivotal and apparently simplest business process – the one for holiday bookings. The first draft of the flow was agreed in less than 15 minutes.

The tool employed is known as a *Swim Lane Diagram* for fairly obvious reasons. It's a little different to other flow-charting approaches in that processes and decisions are grouped by placing them into lanes. In this case, they're arranged horizontally by responsibility. For example, the customer submits a booking request, the sales team checks availability and the finance team processes the payment.

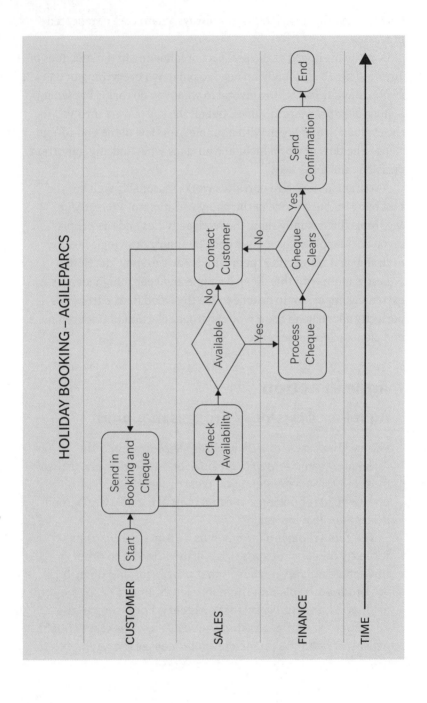

HOLIDAY BOOKING – AGILEPARCS

CUSTOMER

Start → Send in Booking and Cheque

SALES

Check Availability → Available
- No → Contact Customer
- Yes → Process Cheque

FINANCE

Process Cheque → Cheque Clears
- No → Contact Customer
- Yes → Send Confirmation → End

TIME

The session wasn't facilitated and turned into a bit of a meandering free-for-all at times. It overran the allotted hour considerably. Even so, this review of the booking process highlighted several things well worth looking into more closely:

- **Limited options for submitting a booking request:** The only choice currently is by snailmail because of the very low volume of interest but it's peppered with problems and not scalable when business picks up.

- **Only cash and cheque payments are accepted:** Very few customers are able to pay by cash and cheques need to clear before the booking confirmation is sent out. Plus, customers expect more payment flexibility even with a small start-up operation.

- **Too many roles and split responsibilities:** The part-time person who handles the banking and the booking confirmations is only around a couple of mornings each week and this leads to all sorts of processing delays and confusion.

These issues may require substantial time and effort to fully fix. But there are some potential quick workarounds. Getting a credit/debit card reader and agreeing a simpler process for accepting holiday bookings by email are the most obvious.

The flow of work needs to be in an optimum, efficient sequence and must add business value each step along the way. Every situation where this isn't the case is a candidate for improvement. Be on the lookout for any of the following:

- Time lags between steps, especially if they're long or unpredictable.

- Transfers of responsibility where misunderstandings regularly occur.

- Activities that appear unnecessarily complicated.

- Missing must-have functionality or features.
- Anything that's a bit of a mystery.

Just the act of mapping a business process is usually enough to spark fruitful discussions. There's very little chance of it being a waste of time and every chance of it generating a series of eureka moments. And if the current process is pretty much perfect then plenty of praise is deserved as it's such a rare occurrence.

Power of the union

Retrospectives and process-mapping are two specific set pieces where looking to inspect and adapt is very much centre stage. But more importantly, searching for improvements is baked into the day-to-day stuff too. There is a reflective ethos at the heart of *agile* whereby solid ideas are validated and polished up, while half-baked ones are dissected and thought through. The full potential is teased out when there's a communal spirit.

This united approach is a central theme and permeates into everything on offer. Although it's possible for one person to work alone in an *agile way*, the approach is usually a team-based joint activity. From the moment when the *Vision* is first discussed there is a sense of community and a collective determination to get things right. Yes, there will be elements of individual brilliance along the way, but it's primarily a team game.

This doesn't mean the creativity is stifled either – quite the opposite. Blue-sky, left-field thinking is actively encouraged, and *all* ideas are treated with respect. Many innovations evolve from a slightly wacky starting point. There's no danger of going off on a pointless tangent because the team is there for protection from outright madness. There's a freedom of expression and confidence that comes from knowing that someone always has your back.

The desire to inspect and adapt permeates the standard working practices, quite often in a subtle way. As examples, let's take a closer look at the popular technique of peer-to-peer reviews and the widespread use of *Product Demonstrations*:

Peer-to-peer reviews

This is where a colleague, a peer, looks over work-in-progress (WIP) with a fresh pair of eyes. Usually this is done as a final check, but it can be done at any point along the way. This is very different to bringing in a quality assurance specialist (usually an outsider treated with mistrust) to complete an independent review. A peer review is the chance for a colleague with a fresh pair of eyes to spot any glaring errors and to recommend tweaks.

Peer-to-peer reviews are expected to be thorough and robust. They require a climate of trust, mutual respect and honesty. In an *agile* environment this happens with all work of any significance, so the roles are likely to be reversed at some point in the very near future. The unwritten rule is to treat others as you'd want to be treated yourself.

Although these checks aren't considered mandatory, they're an inexpensive way to ensure nothing has been missed or overlooked before a delivery gets handed over to the business community. As a very important part of this review, there are nearly always improvements suggested, usually small tweaks, but sometimes much, much more.

Go *agile* in 15 minutes

Get local feedback

Make the most of the people around you. Ask a colleague for an expert second opinion on an important piece of work-in-progress. It could be a quick proofread of a report, a run-through of a presentation or first thoughts on a new idea, but aim to target a suitable candidate. Provide some guidelines for the review if possible but don't lead the witness.

This final polish can make all the difference. In the spirit of fairness, offer a quid pro quo in return – who knows, the idea might catch on.

Product demonstrations

Keeping the business community engaged is central to the *agile* ethos too, and with this in mind they get frequent demonstrations of the fruits of the team's labours. Someone with close connections to the business usually drives these sessions and shows the stakeholders what's coming very soon. Feedback is encouraged and this is another great way to foster a spirit of collaboration.

Once again, this is carried out in a climate of trust and mutual respect with an open mind regarding the observations made. The stakeholders almost always have additional thoughts on seeing the finished article and there are times when there's been a misunderstanding about a point of detail. This is a review, not a pre-flight check, so comments are normally fed into future plans, except in exceptional circumstances.

The *agile* philosophy is to build towards the final solution, not to try and get it spot on first time. At this late stage, it's recommended to go with what's on offer and feed the suggestions back into the system as candidates for improvements down the line. Usually, previous checks along the way mean only nice-to-haves are uncovered, but if anything's urgent then the next delivery is only a matter of weeks away.

Learn from big fails

Learning from the experience of others is a winner, especially any major mishaps and outright disasters. Tasks, endeavours and projects may have been failing big time for years and usually for the same old reasons. So, it's well worth looking at how *agile* mitigates against the classic big fail scenarios that crop up time and time again.

Late, very late or never arrives

Missed delivery dates is a very common malaise. This is true across the board but especially with the bigger stuff. Sometimes it's a constant series of minor delays, seemingly one step forward and two steps back at times. Or at other times things seem fine right up to the last minute, then a huge delay is announced. Occasionally the train gets cancelled.

This can't happen with *agile*. Work is structured, chunked up and produced in a totally different way which means significant delays are impossible. Instead of putting all the eggs in one basket, smaller chunks are released regularly. It puts an end to the risk of late, very late and cancelled endeavours.

Eye-wateringly expensive

Spiralling costs is another run-of-the-mill malady, and once again the big stuff is the most at risk. Not only a case of a few quid here and there, but quite often a seemingly never-ending series of financial bombshells. As the money pit gets deeper, it gets harder and harder to cut losses and run for the hills.

Once again, big financial meltdowns can't happen with *agile*. An early first delivery checks whether the concept stacks up and funds are invested incrementally from there – only if it does. The option to bail out at any time is built in.

Delivery not as expected

Late deliveries and budget increases are frustrating but it's heart-breaking when the goods arrive, and they're not as expected. This comes in many forms: essential features missing, unwanted features and unnecessary gold-plating, to mention a few of the most common bugbears. In summary, *not fit for the intended purpose* and sometimes as much use as a chocolate teapot.

Yet again, this can't happen with *agile*. Well, in honesty, there might be slight disappointments from time to time but nothing that can't be fixed within a matter of weeks if really necessary. Constant business involvement and incremental deliveries put paid to anything earth-shattering.

Finally, it's worth noting that these biggies are like buses and all come together: spiralling costs, delivery delays and then a disappointing final outcome as the icing on the cake. A huge waste of precious time, hard-earned funds and a massive missed business opportunity.

None of the above can happen when *agile* is implemented in the right way. What more can anyone ask for?

Beware the *agile* improvement tripwires!

Learning from experience is much tougher in practice than it sounds and has its own special pitfalls to manoeuvre. It's a challenge to keep to the guidelines even though they're easy to understand. Steer clear of the following traps:

- **Playing the blame game**: Avoid the temptation to embark on a witch hunt. It's learning reusable lessons that matters, not working out whodunnit.

- **Getting stuck in Groundhog Day**: Be very wary of anything coming up time and time again. Get to the bottom of any re-occurring items and don't set unrealistic targets.

- **Overlooking small tweaks**: Fixing fundamental flaws is brilliant but is bound to be a rare event. Quick wins are the bread and butter of improvements.
- **An occasional nice-to-have**: Avoid treating learning lessons as an optional extra and an added bonus if time permits. For maximum effect, this must be a part of daily life.

The final word

Agile places a big emphasis on learning from experience and being on the lookout for improvements – always wanting to get better at what we do. It's not an afterthought or a nice-to-have, as with some other ways of working, it's built into the how-to mechanics for getting work done – an integral and non-negotiable part of the lifestyle.

There are many processes and techniques on offer to support this, a smorgasbord to choose from. Some, like *Retrospectives*, are almost exclusively geared up to teasing out improvements. With others, like *Product Demonstrations*, it's more of a spin-off. The main thing is that *inspect and adapt* is a central ethos and has been from the early days of *Lean* at Toyota.

It takes time to build up to a position where looking for improvements is part of the daily regime, an almost subconscious activity. Regular set events certainly help to ingrain this as a habit but it's the *agile* spirit of co-operation and collaboration that underpins it more than anything. There's an underlying sense of collective responsibility, a united determination to seek out the positive from whatever life throws at us. This isn't a solo mission – this is a team thing.

Getting to grips with the tools and processes is an important first step. But for optimum results it's essential to constantly get better at what you do and that's an adage that can be applied to everything. Learning from experience and searching for improvements isn't just part of the *agile* lifestyle – it is the *agile* way.

Go *agile* in an hour

Look back and learn

A *Retrospective* is a remarkably straightforward event to execute and is guaranteed to be productive. It serves as a great introduction to a core aspect of *agile* thinking about the importance of learning from experience yet is light on theory. The only pre-requisite is for the participants to have a common area of interest or expertise.

Here are a few easy to follow guidelines:

- Get in an impartial facilitator who won't try to dominate or direct.
- Invite no more than ten people.
- Set a time-box of an hour.
- Ask two questions: What do we do well? What can we do better?
- Focus on actions to promote good practice and prevent the re-occurrence of bad stuff.
- Keep the retro session moving and upbeat and don't get hung up on one or two points.
- Go around the group in turn and list the points raised on a whiteboard or a flipchart.
- Encourage everyone to contribute but use gentle persuasion not strong-arm tactics.
- Allocate a time-box to discuss each point raised but aim for no more than five minutes apiece.
- Schedule a separate, follow-up dedicated session for anything complex to resolve.
- Aim to spend 10 to 20% of the session gathering observations and 80 to 90% discussing them.
- Assign a champion to follow up each recommendation.

This is all about exploring ways to regularise good practice and to avoid things going pear-shaped a second time. The quality of output is the focus, not quantity. The important thing is to generate specific actions. Don't be vague, pin down exactly what's expected and when by.

It's important there's a shared ownership but assign an enthusiastic believer to chase each item.

chapter 4

Use an *agile* mindset for a can-do attitude

"Anyone can train to be a gladiator. What marks you out is having the mind-set of a champion."

Manu Bennett

A sneak preview of Chapter 4

Agile tools and techniques are brilliant but it's the mindset that sets it apart from the crowd – an innovative way of thinking within a positive, can-do culture:

- **Tune into *agile* values and characteristics**: There are traits that underpin *agile* behaviour which can be recognised and nurtured.

- **Promote good behaviour**: There are ways to actively nudge people in the right direction within the daily routine.

- **Build a supportive culture**: Armed with the right mindset, the supporting culture must encourage confidence, self-belief and ambition.

- **Seek expert guidance**: When necessary, mentoring and coaching can fast-track the *agile* process and help avoid classic tripwires.

Be a half-full glass

There are many different ways of working out there, all promising a brighter new tomorrow. There's no cure-all solution, so debates continue to rage about the various pros and the cons of what's on offer. But regardless of the approach preferred, the outlook of the people involved is of paramount importance. Mindsets always make a big difference.

It's easy enough to extol the virtues of a positive outlook but what does that mean in practical terms? It's often a fairly vague notion used during a rallying call or as an aspirational target at salary review time. It's rarely backed up by anything substantial – no checklist of traits that defines the optimum mentality with guidance about how to get there.

Mindset is the final piece of the *agile* golden triangle. The working practices provide the foundation and a learning environment is a wrapper around them. Underpinning all of this is the pursuit of a culture where, among many other things, transparency is the norm and new ideas are embraced. Where an upbeat perspective is pretty much standard.

There's nothing new about being a glass-half-full type of person and for some it will be like a duck taking to water. For others it's a bit of a cultural shift and, as we'll see, there's plenty of supporting help around.

Agile definitions
An *agile* mindset

An *agile* mindset is the way of thinking needed to get the best out of the ways of working. The values, attitudes and behaviours needed for optimum results from the practices and processes. These include many core values such as commitment and flexibility, plus being supportive and always looking to improve.

> *Getting the best out of the tools and processes is very much dependent on having an agile attitude. It's more than a way of working, it's a way of life.*

Encouraging good behaviour

Agile flourishes when there's a can-do vibe and although there's no definitive type of person suited to the lifestyle, there are certain behaviour patterns which are close to mandatory. This isn't about a vague notion of always being positive and looking on the bright side of life – these are traits to help get the job done better. They don't require a personality transplant and are attitudes which can be easily cultivated if the heart is willing:

- **Committed**: Aware of what's achievable and going the extra mile when the going gets tough:
  - Sign-up to stretching, yet realistic, targets.
  - Deliver on promises even if it requires going the extra mile.
  - Dedicated to the cause and determined to get the best out of *agile*.
- **Focussed**: Able to concentrate on what's important and not get distracted by tempting nice-to-haves and general noise:
  - Keep the business end game, the *Vision*, in mind at all times.
  - Consistently deliver business value.
  - Stay *agile* even when the going gets tough.
- **Flexible**: Capable of operating in imperfect conditions and working outside the comfort zone:
  - Adaptable, pushing the boundaries of personal skills.
  - Embrace change when needed instead of fighting against it.
  - Adapt to plan B if things don't go as expected.

- **Courageous**: Not only pushing boundaries and going for it but also not being afraid to fail, as that's bound to happen sometimes too:
  - Think how can it be done rather than it can't be done.
  - Go for what's right and not for what's convenient.
  - Say no to suicide missions.

- **Openness**: Transparent, honest and willing to learn from everything life throws our way:
  - Be transparent even when things aren't going well.
  - Tell it how it is and resist any temptation to spin.
  - Declare issues and any faux pas early on.

- **Respectful**: Polite, courteous and able to see things from the perspective of others:
  - Listen and fully consider other points of view.
  - Treat others as you want to be treated.
  - Remain polite and courteous even when the heat goes up.

- **Challenging**: Thought-provoking and always looking to improve, yet without being aggressive or unnecessarily confrontational:
  - Constantly look for ways to improve and evolve.
  - Question assumptions especially when they are long held.
  - Never coast or rest on past successes.

There are going to be people with a natural disposition who get it immediately, and plenty more who need a bit of time, patience and guidance to get there. If there's plenty of head-nodding when reading this list, it suggests we're off to a flying start – an indicator that the way is an excellent fit. But don't fret if that's not the case, as for the majority going *agile* is a journey.

Setting great expectations

It's essential to build a culture that supports and encourages the target mindset. Individuals won't be committed, focussed, flexible, courageous, open, respectful and challenging if their attitude is frowned upon or even actively discouraged. There's no point in asking people for any of these things if the world around them isn't in tune.

It's best to set the stall out early on with a shared interpretation of all those things that define the intended ways of operating. This common code of practice is best built by the team and bonds them together by defining a shared understanding and commitment. This is not a set of imposed rules and regulations and must never be delivered as a diktat. It's commonly referred to as a *Team Charter*.

Involving the team and agreeing the ground rules, rather than delivering a *fait accompli* guarantees their ownership and buy-in. It's essential to produce the first draft together in a workshop-style way, as the team interactions are almost as important as the output – with considerable debate likely about seemingly straightforward items.

An independent facilitator is much preferred for this, someone with a solid grounding in *agile* and previous experience of producing and using a *Team Charter*. It's not viable to talk about the mindset all the time, so come armed with a series of other prompts to keep the debate moving. Mix it up with direct references and more oblique, culture-related discussions:

Values

Brainstorm the target values to live by. Expect respect and honesty to come up and make sure to throw into the mix focus, commitment and other aspects of the *agile* staple diet we've previously covered. Don't see these as abstract aspirations but explore how the values get translated into working practices. These agreed values are at the heart of the charter.

Behaviours

Include standard good practice, such as *there's no such thing as a stupid question* or *ask questions if ever in doubt*. It's wise to touch on empathy and support, especially in a learning environment. Discuss the scenarios where conduct comes into play to tease out the broader principles. Expect each one to be supported by one or more of the agreed values.

Communication

This isn't solely about the bread and butter decisions of whether to use Slack or WhatsApp for messaging or whether Zoom is better than Google Hangouts for conference calls. Pin down the personal etiquette for messaging, conference calling and emailing – and encourage fast response times with a tolerant attitude to all enquiries.

Meetings

This generic heading covers any get-togethers ranging from the famous *Daily Stand-Ups* through to workshops. Expectations include plenty of common courtesy such as punctuality and not interrupting anyone in full flow. Restrictions on the use of personal tech at meetings are also worth debating up front. This discussion does not include any event-specific logistics, so there's no need to have a rule about the number of toilet breaks.

Responsibilities

Roles are clearly defined in *agile,* especially when using one of the popular frameworks, but it's important to encourage a sense of collective responsibility, especially when things don't go according to plan. Factor in an agreement for any rotating responsibilities and think about holidays and sick leave. The main thing is to deter 'it's not my job' thinking.

Go *agile* in 15 minutes

A personal charter

Discussing a project charter is very much a team event but it's useful to have a think beforehand about things close to your heart, about how you and the people around you operate now and what's needed to be successful in an *agile* world. Draft up ideas to run past the team.

Consider the values you live by and the behaviours you want to encourage. Reflect on the communication channels you use and whether they're suited to an *agile* world. Form a view on who-should-do-what and how to tease the best results out of get-togethers.

It's excellent preparation for the real thing and a chance to probe for any shortfalls in your own world.

The *Team Charter* doesn't need to be all singing and all dancing. Yes, it's about establishing clear working protocols, but the bigger picture is in describing the mindset and culture. Getting everybody singing from the same song sheet and getting everyone thinking along the same lines is the intention, not establishing a comprehensive list of rules to beat people up with.

Doing this when a new team is forming pays big dividends but it's also beneficial when new people join, or as a periodic refresher. In any of these situations, discussing and agreeing the charter bonds the team together, building a shared understanding and commitment. Once in place, the *Team Charter* serves as a useful reminder if anyone strays off the beaten track.

Over time this becomes the accepted way of life and the charter is referred to less frequently. When it works well, it's self-policing with only occasional reminders needed to jog memories, as the monitoring comes from within the gang. It's important to remember that we're not looking for perfect behaviour and occasional lapses are tolerated.

Agile definitions

The onion

A popular visual representation of the *agile* world is in the form of a multi-layered onion. In our version below, the tools and processes, such as the supporting software and workflows, are at the heart of everything.

Wrapped around them are the working practices which include any frameworks in use. Then there are the principles found underpinning the famous *Agile Manifesto* or in our adapted *agile charter* version.

The penultimate layer contains the values, as pinned down in the *Team Charter* before finally, there's the all-important mindset which drives everything and pulls the others together.

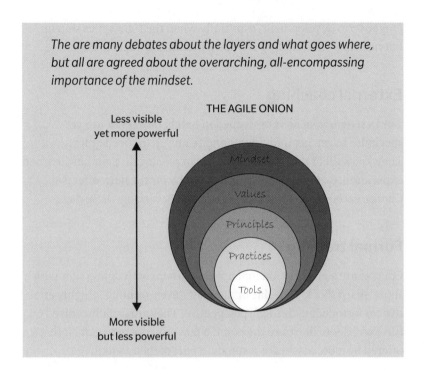

The are many debates about the layers and what goes where, but all are agreed about the overarching, all-encompassing importance of the mindset.

THE AGILE ONION

Less visible
yet more powerful

Mindset

Values

Principles

Practices

Tools

More visible
but less powerful

Getting expert guidance

Changing mindsets and building an *agile* culture is a tough challenge, especially from a standing start. It's hard enough when everyone is as keen as mustard or to the manor born, but the chances are there'll be a few who aren't naturals and others who are not convinced and are sitting on the fence. Without doubt, an expert nudge in the right direction helps:

Internal mentoring

Typically, this is where the more experienced members of the team buddy up with less experienced colleagues. It usually happens naturally within peer reviews and one-to-ones and this type of cross-pollination should be part of the daily regime. It's brilliant for longer-term development, especially when the right types step up, but not viable in fledgling set-ups with limited internal expertise.

External coaching

The best *agile* coaches are steeped in hands-on experience yet specialise in getting individuals and teams up to speed quickly. They know all of the pitfalls and revel in passing on their hard-earned experience. Not the cheapest option but by far the most effective. Choose carefully as the quality is extremely variable these days.

Formal training

Courses are a great option for baptising groups at fledgling sites with a short, sharp shock. Half-day or one-day starter training is highly effective for introducing the *agile* perspective. They are usually centred on fun exercises to illustrate the point, a powerful opening gambit that's offered by most coaches as a standard part of their toolkit.

Agile in action
AgileParcs gets a leg up

The AgileParcs team played it by the book in a bid to get their launch off to a flying start. A local coach was hired to come in to run a half-day introduction for everyone, followed up with another full-day workshop soon after to draft up their *Team Charter*.

There was a degree of nervousness going into the workshop as one of the longest-serving, most experienced and highly vocal employees had some reservations about *agile*. That's a bit of an understatement – the fear was there might be an anti, negative vibe.

Somewhat unexpectedly this helped focus the attention of everyone in the workshop, especially during the discussion about behaviours and values. Deft facilitating was a factor, but the rest of the team were galvanised into a vocal pro counterposition.

It was a bumpy ride. By the end of the session, the charter was in pretty decent shape considering it was a first draft. Of equal importance were the discussions and debates.

Fight off the temptation to go it alone on the back of one-day primer and a bit of additional reading. The most effective way to get off on the right foot is to get access to a coach. Learning to drive would be a decent analogy. Self-teaching based on observation and internet research is viable but it's a route full of potholes. You'll get far better results with the help of a qualified instructor.

Investing in *agile* coaching from the off mitigates against going seriously off-track and pays for itself. Common faux pas are avoided and the ramp-up time is shortened considerably. As this will be a key appointment, it pays dividends to recruit carefully. Get someone in to facilitate the *Team Charter*, and it will soon become obvious whether they know their onions.

An essential aspect of the coach's remit is to build up internal capabilities. Coaching isn't intended to be a long-term gig. The best coaches aim to make themselves redundant, so be wary of anyone more interested in maintaining their income stream. Expect involvement to be regular and intense at the start but to taper off within months. There's nothing wrong with periodic health checks thereafter but avoid staying in long-term intensive care.

Building a supporting culture

Anyone armed with a positive mindset is on the right road, but it makes all the difference when there's a supportive culture. The wrong conditions hinder enormously, as anyone who operates in the blame game knows from harsh experience. Equally, a conducive operating environment helps immeasurably. It's so much easier swimming with the tide rather than against it.

Achieving the right set-up doesn't require a mass conversion to the *agile* way – although that would be lovely of course. It's more about the local eco system supporting certain ways of thinking and operating. There are two standout aspects for *agile* to be successful: empowering the team to get the job done and ensuring the business is actively engaged. Without either, it's an uphill battle.

There are many influences on an *agile* culture, but few are in the same league as team empowerment and business engagement. They are the bookends that keep everything else in good order.

Team empowerment

This is having the autonomy to get on with things without continually referring back to a higher authority for approval. It might sound a bit scary but for many it's not hugely dissimilar to what already goes on. The end goal, the *Vision*, is the guiding light but the day-to-day decisions about the actual doing is left to the workers.

Streamlining the decision-making process speeds up the delivery process without devaluing the quality. The business decides what they want, and the team decide how to do it. This is a sensible demarcation with each doing what comes naturally. This might seem to be a bit risky but in practice it's not, because transparency ensures that the business is always in the loop.

This must be real empowerment and not only the ability to make minor, less critical decisions. Nor can decisions get reviewed and overruled. No need for nerves as there are plenty of in-built controls that prevent things from going horribly wrong. Everything to gain and nothing to lose.

Business engagement

Team empowerment doesn't mean the business can define the *Vision* and then walk away. Quite the contrary. *Agile* expects the business community to have skin in the game and a vested interest at all times. This involvement comes in many forms, shapes and sizes but it is ever-present in some form or another.

Once the *Vision* is nailed down, the business plays a vital part in translating it into the component parts (the *User Stories*), plus it drives the prioritisation and shapes the *MVP*. A comprehensive package which is usually channelled through one representative – the *Product Owner (PO)*. Plenty of *agile*-speak, but in essence copious direct and indirect business involvement.

All communications are channelled through the *Product Owner* on a day-to-day basis, but that doesn't mean the business community is totally hands-off. All deliveries are showcased to the wider group before the D-day and this provides final confirmation that all's well. If not, there's an opportunity for frank discussions and a joint decision about the way forward.

Beware *agile* mindset tripwires!

Agile life isn't only about encouraging the good, it's also about avoiding the bad. There are *anti-agile* patterns to look out for, those things that go against the grain and are highly counter-productive. Don't expect Peter or Priscilla Perfect but watch out for anyone who is regularly going against the flow:

- **Adverse to change**: Preferring stability, or wanting to stay in a comfort zone, is seriously inhibiting.

- **Looking for failure**: There's nothing wrong with assessing the risks but let's not see disaster around every corner.

- **Regularly disruptive**: When challenging everything, even the core concepts, becomes the norm.

- **Lone wolf mentality**: Wanting to do things on their own and without interacting with anyone else.

- **Avoiding *agile***: Giving plenty of excuses for bypassing standard practice and procedures.

> *Be extremely wary of anyone with a full set of flaws, especially if they're highly vocal. This is typified by a general anti-stance on everything and continually sidestepping the spirit of the Team Charter. One very bad apple can spoil the barrel.*

The final word

Agile processes provide a fantastic foundation, but success doesn't solely depend on having brilliant methods. Mindset is equally important to get the best results – having the wrong outlook can massively throttle what can be achieved. In fairness, that's true of almost anything in life but it's especially applicable to *agile*.

Other approaches tend to pay little attention to mindset and the surrounding culture, concentrating exclusively on reams and reams of step-by-step guidance on the how-to-do mechanics. *Agile*, in contrast, promotes a can-do culture steeped in collaboration. This positive, proactive attitude is imbedded into the practices and encouraged in the wider philosophy.

Not everyone is a perfect fit and, as a general rule, people bring all sorts of personal quirks to the table. The key is in building a glass-half-full culture and encouraging a collective spirit which helps brings out the best in everyone. We're not in search of perfection but are hell-bent on encouraging traits known to help *agile ways* to become ingrained as habits.

Don't expect everyone to be transformed into a superstar overnight. Expect teething pains and be careful when things are seriously not right. Ignoring persistent anti-patterns and anti-*agile* behaviour will seriously damage your *agile* health.

Go *agile* in an hour

Build the *Team Charter*

A *Team Charter* underpins the mindset and culture. It sets out a collective agreement up front and serves as a reminder whenever needed later on. Discussing and drafting the Charter is a vital part of the process, when hearts and minds are won over.

Get all the team involved in this. If possible, get a pukka coach in for the session but as this is a one-hour exercise, a pragmatic compromise is to find an impartial facilitator. Come prepared with an outline format but spend a couple of minutes checking the team are on board (but no more).

There's no set format for a Charter but be sure to consider values and behaviours initially. If they get covered off and agreed, then consider it a good day's work. Time permitting, move onto communication and/or meetings:

- **Values**: Reflect on the values you want to live by. Well worth considering respect, honesty, focus and commitment.

- **Behaviours**: There's no such thing as a stupid idea here – hey, that can even be one of the recommendations!

- **Communication**: What are the channels that are currently used and are they suitable for the world you want?

- **Meetings**: Include any sort of get-togethers, covering etiquettes and procedures but not hard logistics.

This is about nurturing an agile culture and mindset, not an attempt to define a rulebook. And it's fine to set the bar high but keep it achievable.

chapter 5

———

Where to start – try *Kanban* or *Scrum*

"Be stubborn about your goals and flexible about your methods."

Anon

A sneak preview of Chapter 5

Get off to a very fast, totally stress-free launch by using one of the perfectly formed frameworks on offer.

- **You're spoilt for choice:** There are several excellent varieties available, but *Kanban* and *Scrum* are up there with the best.
- *Kanban* **is simple yet powerful:** Easy to get to grips with, yet powerful and flexible. Getting started is a breeze.
- *Scrum* **is popular and fully featured:** More effort up front but massively worth it. Especially fab with bigger missions.
- **Two great options:** *Kanban* is very safe and surprisingly flexible, while *Scrum* is a feature-rich, comprehensive package. Look no further.

Getting started

Once the decision is made to go *agile* – or to at least *give* it a whirl – the big question is simply where to begin. There are plenty of excellent routes in, but without doubt the quickest and safest way is to utilise one of the popular *agile* frameworks. There are several choices and the good news is they're all fully formed, tried and tested and a very fast start is guaranteed.

We're going to concentrate on getting up and running with two excellent options: *Kanban* and *Scrum*. Both are hugely popular, and rightly so. Both provide everything you need in one handy box. *Kanban* is brilliantly easy to get to grips with but there's more to it than meets the eye. *Scrum* is probably the most widely known *agile* framework and although there's more to get your head around, there's nothing to fret about. Both can be used pretty much anywhere.

We'll step through the essence of *Kanban* and *Scrum* and help you to pick the best fit. Each has its own nuances, but both do the job superbly well, plus they're backed by extensive resources and support networks. Having to choose between two excellent options is a nice situation to be in.

Kanban basics

Kanban 看板 means signboard in Japanese and it came to life as a method to fine-tune and improve the production line at the car giant Toyota. Partly to help balance customer demand with build capacity and partly to improve the handling of assembly bottlenecks. Over time it has been taken up in a variety of other business sectors to improve their workflows and is now one of the fastest growth areas in the *agile* arena.

Kanban hasn't strayed from its 1950s roots. The simplicity and ease of executing the underpinning ideas remains a big attraction. Although there's a built-in respect for how the job gets done at the moment, there's also an implicit determination to pursue incremental change – to make current work processes better, little by little. *Kanban* is about evolution, not revolution.

It's easy to grasp, simple to implement and has negligible running costs. The launch pad is whatever you do right now, so there's no blocker to an immediate start. There are two main steps for pinning down the status quo:

- **Picture the current workflow:** Begin by producing a visual representation of the flow of work, from when things are ready to go right through to job complete. Define the key steps along the way but don't be tempted to go overboard with detail. It must be easy to comprehend.

- **Control the workflow progress:** How work progresses from step to step in the workflow must be clear, with a check at the end of each one to validate it's fine to move on. It includes specific guidance on how to judge whether a piece of work is ready to start and how to confirm it is complete.

This analysis of how things are done now is at the epicentre of *Kanban*. Usually it's not hard to do and it's reasonable to expect it to be drafted within hours. If it takes days then that's food for thought in itself. Let's see how it's done.

Visualise the workflow

When mapping the flow of work, don't get hung up on the detail. Think big picture for the basic end-to-end format. What are the generic states along the way applicable to everything you do? By far the simplest, most popular and arguably the purest workflow consists of just three: things to do, those in progress and finally work done. When first launching *Kanban* it's well worth beginning there and adding more if you feel the need:

- To do – when what's wanted is clear and ready to go.
- In progress – once work is assigned and actively progressing.
- Done – finished and ready for the business to use as they see fit.

Once the workflow is visualised, it can be mapped directly onto a *Kanban* board. The board is a graphic representation of the end-to-end flow and can be held electronically but as discussed before it's very effective to start with a physical wallboard, located in the heart of all the corporate action. Either way, a series of columns represents the flow of work from to do through to done.

Agile in action

AgileParcs goes *Kanban*

The AgileParcs team considered all the options before deciding to keep their flow simple. The first draft contained five distinct states – To Do, Design, Build, Commission and Done – but the feeling was that a couple of them didn't apply all the time. By a very narrow majority it was agreed to keep it simple initially.

In their world, the important, common distinctions are simply: when tasks are ready to go (to do), when work is cracking on (in progress), or once it's dusted off (done).

The full shooting match isn't defined but there's enough to test the concept in the upcoming Easter holidays, with a bit of time to adapt to feedback before the summer season. Priorities can be shuffled right up until work starts on the next task.

All the stories on their Kanban board are a stepping stone to the AgileParcs end game, but also deliver business value in their own right.

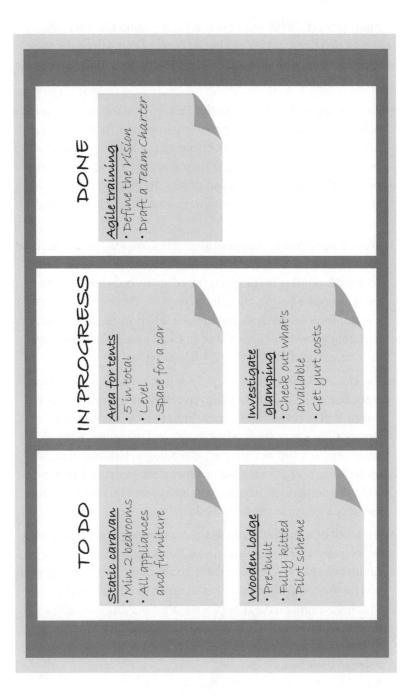

TO DO

Static caravan
- Min 2 bedrooms
- All appliances and furniture

Wooden lodge
- Pre-built
- Fully fitted
- Pilot scheme

IN PROGRESS

Area for tents
- 5 in total
- Level
- Space for a car

Investigate glamping
- Check out what's available
- Get yurt costs

DONE

Agile training
- Define the vision
- Draft a Team Charter

In many respects, *agile* work management is similar across the leading disciplines and we've already covered end-to-end delivery mechanics in detail. However, there are subtle, yet vitally important aspects of *Kanban* that make it unique:

- **Jobs are allocated dynamically:** This is one of the most distinctive points about working in a *Kanban* environment. Teams adopt a 'what's next policy'. The work item with the highest priority is pulled into play when the next person becomes available. Priorities can change at any time and that's fully embraced in a *Kanban* environment. Thus, the team can respond rapidly to changing business demands.

- **Work-in-progress is capped:** Trying to do too many things at the same time is counterproductive, so with *Kanban* there's a limit set for the number of things on the go at any one time. For practical reasons, it's best to allow for a couple of concurrent tasks per person, three at the most, but the aim is to prevent anyone accumulating a treasure trove of half-finished jobs. This encourages everyone to be a finisher, not a job hoarder.

- *Backlog* **reviewed frequently:** By definition *Backlogs* are never static but with *Kanban* they're even more effervescent. It's not unheard of to review it on a daily basis and even last-minute negotiations are possible when there's an emergency. Even so, it's important to avoid a culture of responding to half-baked ideas and whims. *User Stories* must always be adequately formed even if they're desperately urgent. Regular assessments underpin the mood of a dynamic yet controlled environment.

- **All work of a similar size:** As a general principle it's a good idea to keep *User Stories* lean and mean. Breaking work down into smaller chunks wherever possible avoids huge, long-running jobs and *Kanban* actively encourages slimmer, similar-sized slices. This helps regulate the flow of work, thus making it easier to predict end-to-end cycle times and the availability of resources. Of course, whatever size, all packages must still deliver business value in their own right.

Go *agile* in 15 minutes

Download and play with a *Kanban* app

Download the popular *Kanban* workflow app Trello on to a smartphone, tablet or whatever is your electronic fancy. The basic version is free and more has more than enough functionality to get going. It's easy to use with plenty of online help available (check out the Trello 101 guidance for back-to-basics).

Set up as many *Kanban* boards as you want – there's no limit. Perhaps one for personal stuff and another one for work stuff. Within each, create the columns you want (*lists* in Trello-speak) and a good opener is To do, In progress and Done. Add your tasks (called *cards*) and hey presto, you're off.

If Trello doesn't appeal, then search for free Kanban board apps. You'll be amazed at the choice.

A huge selling point is the ramp-up speed from a standing start – no more than a couple of days if enough effort is put in. There's no risk of waiting for months before finding out if *Kanban* is a good match. Days, or a couple of weeks at the most, is enough to get a gut feel. In the very unlikely event of it turning into a total debacle it's easy to revert back to the old ways, so the overall risk rating is extremely low.

Introducing *Scrum*

Scrum is an extremely popular option for going *agile*. It's in fashion for a host of excellent reasons but the best one is simply that it's easy to use and works brilliantly. Its framework provides structure without going overboard, which is no mean feat. Roles are clearly defined, yet come with enough flexibility to avoid stifling creative thinking and innovation. The package is fun to work within and brings the best out of people, which is an enticing combination.

There's a bit more to *Scrum* but it's still easy to implement and has the advantage of being well suited to projects, even big ones. Within the framework there's detailed guidance on all aspects of who-does-what but it's with a deft touch that doesn't stifle innovation or creativity. It comes with a fully formed support network, and an unprecedented generosity and willingness to help abound.

As would be expected, *Scrum* is firmly focused on delivering incrementally in a series of useable chunks. The very first of these is the absolute minimum to get going and then the rest is layered on top from there. Every one of these increments is effectively a mini project, known as a *Sprint* – a fixed-length time-box of one, two, three or four weeks.

A very popular option is two weeks, and although there's no recommended duration, many people feel one week is too short and four is far too long. *Sprints* provide a regular flow of product to the business team so don't be tempted to vary the duration apart from in exceptional circumstances. Get into a groove and maintain a regular cadence. With the timescale fixed, the only variable is what can be delivered in that period of time.

But before we take a closer look at how that pans out on a day-to-day basis, let's look first at how the roles and responsibilities within the *Scrum* team are set up.

Let's get self-organised

It will come as no surprise that *Scrum* keeps it simple when it comes to responsibilities. There are only three roles: *Product Owner, Scrum Master* and *Team Member*. There are always several *Team Members* but only one each of the other two. The defining traits of a *Scrum* team are self-organising, self-starting and self-governing.

There are different opinions about the optimum team size, but the recommended min/max is between three and nine. A much more important consideration is for this unit to have all the skills needed to get the job done. There's a collective onus on the gang to pull together and deliver, whatever it takes.

Product Owner – the business eyes and ears

The *Product Owner* (*PO*) is the business representative in every respect and looks after their interests on a day-to-day basis. This covers everything from shaping what's needed, to confirming that deliveries are as expected. It doesn't stop there either as the *PO* also represents the needs of the end customer too. They're responsible for delivering business value to both their own organisation and to the end users.

The *Product Owner* will be lobbied by everyone about priority calls but ultimately, what they say goes. It's not only about being decisive – the ability to balance off conflicting views and being tactful is important too. In addition to everything else, wisdom and negotiation skills are both needed. This is a pivotal role that is measured by the quality of the list of prioritised requirements (the *Backlog*), which is the spine for any *Scrum* team.

Even when the *Backlog* is in good shape, the team will have plenty of questions and the *Product Owner* needs to be freely available on a day-to-day basis. In parallel, it's important for the *PO* and the team to build up a buffer of requirements to avoid living from hand to mouth. Ideally, the aim is a *Backlog* with a depth of at least a couple of *Sprints* at all times.

A day in the life of a *Product Owner*

- Preparing new *User Stories*
- Answering questions about work in progress
- Keeping the stakeholders in the loop and happy
- Homing in on the *Product Vision* at all times.

   It looks easy enough on paper but requires a skilful touch and a clear understanding of where the business wants to go.

Scrum Master – a facilitator and enabler

The *Scrum Master* does everything imaginable to help the team perform to the best of their abilities. Part of the job involves practical day-to-day stuff such as facilitating team gatherings. Part is about overseeing the run-of-the-mill logistics such as getting the right people in the right place at the right time. Part is about removing blockers and greasing the team wheels.

The *Scrum Master* provides vital support to the *Product Owner* and helps promote a culture where the *Backlog* stays in good shape at all times. When the *PO* is thinking ahead and the rest of the team are focusing on the *Sprint* obligations, the *Scrum Master* helps maintain the tricky balance between short-term commitments and future aspirations.

The *Scrum Master* is ultimately responsible for maintaining the best possible environment for the team to operate within and to help their work lives run smoothly. But not at any cost, as the *Scrum Master* is the custodian of the *Scrum* process, making sure that things are done the right way.

A day in the life of a *Scrum Master*

- Facilitating the *Scrum Events* and other get-togethers
- Minimising distractions for the team
- Removing blockers to progress
- Helping the team to stay on the path

  It's harder than it might seem to steer the team without becoming dogmatic, nit-picking or appearing highhanded.

The *Development Team* – the engine room

The rest of the squad is usually referred to collectively as the *Development Team*. Each individual is known by the rather bland title of *Team Member*, but the role is rich and diverse. They're all multi-talented, multi-disciplined and ultimately in control of their own destiny. Once the *Product Owner* sets out their stall in the *Backlog*, the *Development Team* works out how best to do it.

Within the confines of each *Sprint*, the team are self-managing and focused on delivering end results – taking prioritised items from the *Backlog* and turning them into working artefacts. They are trusted to operate as sensible grown-ups who can get on with it without needing micro-management.

Scrum in action

At the epicentre of the *Scrum* framework are four key events properly known as *Scrum Events*, but very often referred to as *Scrum Ceremonies*. All play a vital part and each one is totally indispensable. Fully assembled they form the end-to-end structure of each *Sprint*:

- **Sprint Planning:** This happens at the very beginning and does exactly what is says on the tin. This is where the final decisions are made about what business requirements – usually in the form of *User Stories* – are going into the *Sprint*. The *Product Owner* comes armed with prioritised requirements and the team forecast how much they can handle in the next *Sprint*.

- **Daily Scrum:** This is where the team huddle together and bring their colleagues up to date on what they've been doing, what they plan to do and report any roadblocks. This happens every day without exception. This enables the team to be on the same page and have a joint plan for the next 24 hours. It's certainly not a status update to the *Scrum Master*.

- **Sprint Review:** This takes place at the end of the *Sprint* when the *Product Owner* with support from the team showcases the business-centric work to the stakeholders – when things pan out as expected, this is whatever the team forecasted they'd deliver during *Sprint* planning. This is primarily a final pre-launch check and really keeps the wider business in the loop.

- **Team Retrospective:** This is a look back on the *Sprint* and highlights the things that went well and anything that could be improved. Whatever the outcome, there's usually a mix of recommendations to take forward to the next *Sprint*. It's important to focus on the big winners and quality is more important than quantity. *The Scrum Master* facilitates, and the team drive the recommended improvements.

There are no nice-to-haves in this collection. Each *Sprint* must start with planning and end with a review topped off by a team *Retrospective*. Every day there must be a *Daily Scrum* (or *Daily Stand-Up* as it's commonly referred to). If any of these appear surplus to requirements, then something's going seriously wrong.

Sprint planning – setting out the stall

As each *Sprint* is a mini project in its own right, it will come as no great surprise that it kicks off with a planning session where the team agree what's to be done. Planning in this context is an interactive event to review the prioritised *User Stories* that are ready to go and decide how many can be delivered within the next *Sprint*.

The *Product Owner* brings along a wish list that is invariably more than can be achieved in one time-box and the team decide what can be done based on experience. The end target must be challenging but achievable and the team always have the final say on when they have reached full capacity. The sum of the parts is expressed as the *Sprint Goal*, a pithy declaration of immediate intent which is a step towards the *Vision*.

There are times when planning goes very smoothly, usually when the *Backlog* is rock solid, and the team is clear about their projected capacity. Then it's a straightforward case of the team selecting stories, one by one, that they're confident of finishing to done status. It isn't always straightforward though and usually there's a sympathetic negotiation between the *Product Owner* and the team, with the *Scrum Master* facilitating.

The end result is the team forecasting delivery of a subset of the prepared stories which is then dubbed the *Sprint Backlog*. At this point the team must be clear about what they're getting themselves into and the *Product Owner* must be satisfied with the intended outcome. There's a mutual interest in getting this right and ensuring the contract is a fair one.

Once the *User Stories* that make up the *Sprint Backlog* are finalised, then it's over to the *Development Team* to get on with it. The thinking and preparation are over – all systems go!

Agile in action

AgileParcs planning disaster

Planning sessions aren't always plain sailing and it would be fair to say that the first AgileParcs *Sprint* planning ceremony didn't go well at all.

The session was in trouble before it even started because the new *Product Owner* couldn't get enough *User Stories* ready in time. A couple were in a reasonable state, but the most important stuff was in poor shape. The business requirements were a bit vague with questions remaining about pivotal points.

The *Scrum Master* compounded the problem by taking a laissez-faire approach to the ensuing debacle. Then, despite feeling uncomfortable and voicing reservations, the *Development Team* felt pressurised into accepting the stories as is and optimistically hoped to sort out the requirements on the go.

The planning session ran for twice as long as expected and by the end tempers were frayed. The team felt that some of the important half-baked tickets might be fatally flawed and decided to take in a few extra tickets they preferred the look of.

A perfect storm is brewing.

Daily Scrum – keeping in touch

The *Daily Scrum* or *Daily Stand-Up*, as it's popularly referred to, is a time-boxed, mini-meeting that lasts no more than 15 minutes and happens every day without fail. It's an opportunity for each *Team Member* to update their colleagues and report anything blocking progress towards the *Sprint Goal*. The backdrop is the *Sprint* task board which should be prominently available for reference.

The recommended format is blisteringly straightforward with each *Team Member* in turn answering the same three questions:

- What did you do yesterday? A summary not a blow-by account.

- What will you do today? Again, only an overview of intent.

- What impediments do you have? Anything obstructing progress.

Sprints rarely run totally smoothly, and hiccups are to be expected. Therefore, an important aspect of this assembly is to get any blockers out in the open. Issues are tabled but not normally solved on the spot – the *Scrum Master* has the responsibility for sussing out a way forward. The plan is to line up a helping hand and avoid issues becoming a damaging distraction.

Despite the simplicity of the format, even in a mature *Scrum* environment these sessions don't always run smoothly. Occasional detours are to be expected. Ditto for overruns. But if they're regularly dysfunctional it's a serious warning sign.

Agile in action
AgileParcs daily debacle

It's not easy to keep everyone on message at the *Daily Scrum*, especially in the early days when the team are finding their feet. It's fair to say that the AgileParcs team struggled more than most.

Even rounding up the team at the same time was challenging. At least one late arrival each day led to a mixture of delayed starts, updates getting repeated and occasional incomplete reporting because of total no-shows.

The sessions regularly went off piste with blow-by-blow updates and lengthy discussions of all and everything. As time went on it was easy to see certain people were getting bored, irritated and switching off. For some it soon became a box-ticking exercise rather than anything constructive.

The *Scrum Master* failed to nip bad behaviour in the bud, compounding problems by conducting investigations and complaining about slow progress. Very soon the *Daily Stand-Up* was often an acrimonious battleground.

Anyone observing a couple of AgileParcs daily disasters would see there's definitely trouble at t'mill.

Sprint Review – delivering the goods

Keeping the stakeholders permanently in the loop is a massive part of the *agile* ethos and this happens on a day-to-day basis because of the constant involvement of the *Product Owner*. But there's wider business contact at the end of each *Sprint* when the *Product Owner* shows off the fruits of the team's labour to the business stakeholders.

This is another *Sprint* Ceremony, called the *Sprint Review*. It's open to all stakeholders and interested parties within reason.

This session is facilitated by the *Scrum Master*, but the team and the *Product Owner* are very much centre stage. They showcase their wares in whatever format makes most sense to the audience, preferably demoed as the end product will eventually be used. Each individual *User Story* is laid bare, warts 'n all if necessary. Full disclosure is what's expected in this context.

It's about much more than showing the stakeholders what they're getting. When executed well, the *Sprint Review* brings everyone together with a sense of collective ownership and a common goal. Not only the final nod on whether the deliveries are fit-for-purpose, but also confirming they're another step towards the promised land. This is a sea change from long waits and a you-get-what-you-get culture.

Most of the time, this leaves everyone with a warm satisfied feeling which is excellent for building confidence. It's normal for minor issues and small oversights to be revealed under the spotlight but with *agile* a problem shared is a problem solved. And if a bit of fine-tuning is urgently needed, the next delivery is only a matter of weeks away.

Agile tips

Running effective review sessions

Don't be shy when it comes to running *Sprint Reviews*. Always invite the relevant stakeholders, of course, but see if a couple of movers and shakers can be tempted along too occasionally. Build on the natural buzz and use these events to promote the world of *agile* and *Scrum*.

Pay attention to getting the logistics right. The *Scrum Master* needs to book a fit-for-purpose, well-equipped room in advance and get there early on the day to check it's ready to go. There's only one chance to make a good first impression and there's nothing better than getting off to a seamless, trouble-free start.

The *Scrum Master* is the facilitator, not the centre of attention. The team are all present for a very good reason and each is expected to play their part in some way or other:

- Set the scene by confirming the format of the review and introducing the team.
- Restate the *Sprint Goal* as agreed up front during the *Sprint* planning.
- Demo each *User Story* in whatever way to make sense to the audience and in a logical sequence.
- Encourage feedback without promising too much in the heat of the moment.
- Ratify each sign-off as you go along and reiterate any agreed caveats.
- Get the *Product Owner* and stakeholders to confirm the team has met the original *Sprint Goal*.
- Look forward by sharing and discussing the intended focus of the next *Sprint*.
- Announce the arrangements for the next review, close the session and enjoy the moment.

Be prepared but don't over rehearse – it's not a National Theatre production. Put all your cards on the table and never be tempted to be economical with the truth or resort to smoke and mirrors.

There are times when *Sprint Reviews* are very straightforward and over with little fuss, but these are few and far between. Even when the team sets out their stall clearly during planning, there are bound to be questions and niggles when the stakeholders run their final pre-flight checks. It's normal for minor tweaks and future improvements to be suggested. Quite often there are debates about points of detail and that's absolutely fine too.

The *Sprint Review* is when everything comes together. The journey started with the *Product Vision* and then a slice pops out at the *Sprint Review*. This is a great litmus test and when all is going well generally it's obvious during these sessions. Conversely, if things are not so rosy then this is when the tell-tale warning signs appear.

Retrospectives

Before jumping onto the next *Sprint* rollercoaster, the team gets together to reflect on how things panned out in the current one. This is called a *Retrospective* and it's the final non-negotiable ceremony. It must take place whether things went well or badly, as there's as much to be learned from good practice as there is from a debacle. Never be tempted to give this a miss and plough straight on.

The groundwork begins early on as the search for improvements must be at the back of everyone's mind at all times. Encourage the team to note down their thoughts whenever they occur – no need for chapter and verse as a couple of sentences will be enough as a memory jogger at the *Retrospective* itself. Less is more in this respect.

Getting the team to open up is never easy and translating their comments into realisable actions is a skill that takes time to fully master. It's true to say that most observations are going to be about learning from mistakes but it's important to keep an eye out for good behaviour that can repeated too. For *Scrum*, this is the epicentre for process improvements and we've already covered how important that is to the *agile* lifestyle.

Agile in action

AgileParcs retro tour de force

Against all the odds it was a pretty decent *Sprint*, as the AgileParcs team delivered some good quality product with plenty of business value. The mood was generally positive at the *Retrospective*, all things considered. Just a touch of disappointment bubbling about failing to deliver several *User Stories*.

The team stuck with their normal format and asked the standard questions: *what went well* and *what could be improved?* The session meandered at times and significantly overran the agreed time-box of an hour. Many points were discussed but the team pinpointed five key things they wanted to focus on during the next *Sprint*.

Each of the main points was assigned a champion, with the expectation of seeing progress by their next session:

1 **Create better quality *User Stories***: Many of the issues faced in the *Sprint* were tracked back to poorly defined require- ments. More time was recommended for thinking things through in advance and building a more robust *Backlog*.

2 **Be more considered during *Sprint* planning**: An over opti- mistic view on what the team could do led to a completely unrealistic forecast. It was agreed to only take in fully formed requirements and to be realistic about capacity.

3 **Focus on the business' highest priorities**: A few very inter- esting but low priority requirements were picked up before the more important stuff. This will be an easy one to fix by strictly adhering to the designated running sequence.

4 **Stick to the script at the daily gatherings**: Late arrivals and going off topic were a couple of the reasons identified for overruns during the *Daily Scrums*. Hence an agreement to re-focus on: *what have you done, what are you going to do* and *are there any blockers?*

The openness, honesty and determination to learn from expe- rience during the *Retrospective* spoke volumes. The recom- mendations generated went to the heart of the matter and it was sensible to limit attention to only four key items. Building a perfect world by the end of the next *Sprint* wasn't realistic but starting the journey was spot on.

> *In the next Sprint the Daily Scrums were dragged back on track and much more time was invested into developing solid stories. Lessons were learned.*

Maintaining a regular heartbeat

With *Scrum* the days of waiting around for once-in-a-blue-moon deliveries are long gone. Instead of endlessly anticipating the arrival of all and everything, smaller chunks of business value are delivered based on a set schedule – fixed-length increments set at one, two, three or four weeks. The regular arrival of another piece of the jigsaw is invariably a breath of fresh air.

A reliable delivery cadence is the trademark of a performing *Scrum* team. There's nothing more potent for building business confidence than when there's an understanding about what's coming next and when it will arrive. It gets the business into a habit of expecting product and is a big factor in keeping their buy-in. It does put a degree of pressure on the team but it's a positive challenge.

The timing isn't a vague commitment, it's very precise. For example, every two weeks means exactly that, let's say every other Wednesday. The number of *User Stories* delivered each time may vary but the arrival dates are guaranteed and can be plugged into diaries up front. The *Vision* is delivered in pieces that are useful in their own right.

Although weekly deliveries are exciting, there's a limit to what can be done in such a short timescale and the business team barely have time to pause for breath. Every four weeks permits meatier content, but it can seem a long wait. No surprise then that the most popular format is every two. It's a perfect balance.

A piece-by-piece approach revolutionises the relationship between the doers and the receivers. It provides regular, concrete evidence that things are on the right track, which is far more reassuring than any project status report. In fact, it's a sign of *Scrum* working well when the business starts to complain because they must wait *weeks* for what they want.

A complete end-to-end solution

Scrum guidance is concise without being constraining, with excellent specialist advice widely available in many formats. It's extremely easy to get started. Sticking to the events and operating within the recommended team structure are non-negotiable and the rest flows from there.

Go *Agile* in 15 minutes

Read the *Scrum Guide*

Ken Schwaber and Jeff Sutherland are the founding fathers of *Scrum* and they created a pithy summary cunningly called the *Scrum Guide*. It's kept up to date, but changes are few and far between. Downloads are freely available at www. Scrumguides.org.

Only 16 pages including a cover page and the table of contents, so no valid excuses for giving it a swerve.

Scrum is a fully formed *agile* bundle for transforming what the business team wants into end product. The only word of warning from experienced practitioners is that getting the best out of the framework requires a deft touch and the right mindset. So, for exceptional results, remember to stick with all the advice we've covered.

There's something reassuring about a framework which can be perfectly summed up in one diagram:

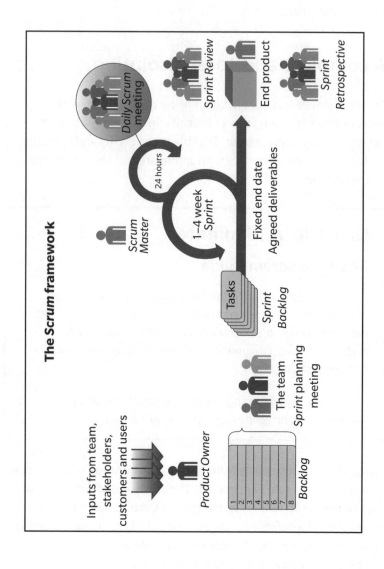

The Scrum framework

Inputs from team, stakeholders, customers and users

Product Owner

Backlog

The team

Sprint planning meeting

Scrum Master

Daily Scrum meeting

24 hours

1–4 week Sprint

Tasks

Sprint Backlog

Fixed end date
Agreed deliverables

Sprint Review

End product

Sprint Retrospective

Various variations

When it comes to ways of working, there are many intriguing variations to be found in the *agile* world. The community has been debating various blended and hybrid approaches recently and *ScrumBan* (a combination of *Scrum* and *Kanban*) is one of the best known. However, there's a range of opinions about how effective these fusions are and it's one of the hottest of hot potatoes.

As part of our more targeted focus on *Scrum* and *Kanban*, it's worth mentioning there are plenty of practitioners who draw on the intent of the other framework with great success. In particular, when *Kanban* teams reuse elements of *Scrum*:

- *Retrospectives*: Essentially, *inspecting and adapting* the work-flow. The timing of sessions is not fixed with *Kanban* but it's equally valuable to ask the same questions: what do we do well and what can we do better?

- *Daily Stand-Up*: If nothing else, raising the profile of any imped-iments justifies a daily get-together with *Kanban* too. It also underpins the sense of teamwork and general collaboration that's important to preserve.

- **Planning:** *Kanban* is more focussed on just-in-time activities but there are times when it pays to think ideas through in advance, with input from representatives from all the relevant disciplines.

- **Reviews:** There's no set-piece show and tell events with *Kanban*, but timely feedback is part of the ethos. Pre-launch mini reviews make good sense whatever framework you use to do the work.

- **Roles:** *Kanban* doesn't specify roles but it's worth thinking about what the *Product Owner* and the *Scrum Master* do. There will still be a need to involve the business, and the team will have blockers to resolve.

Kanban & Scrum
in a Nutshell

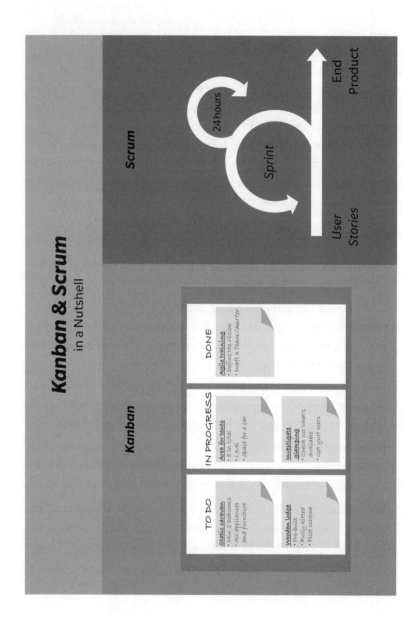

Kanban versus *Scrum*

Both are brilliant. Both are steeped in *agile* thinking. Both have their pros and cons. Spoilt for choice is the phrase that regularly comes to mind. More importantly, it's quite likely one will suit your world better than the other. Contemplate the options before jumping in but don't overthink it.

Kanban's strengths

- Builds from the status quo
- Zero risk and minimal cost
- Dynamic prioritising and scheduling
- Brings structure to unconnected tasks
- *An agile* fast start

Kanban's weaknesses

- Not the best option for big projects

The Kanban framework won't let you down, the only risk is a poorly executed implementation. It's a fantastic way to experience agile as opposed to reading about it.

Scrum's strengths

- Fully formed, comprehensive support
- Low start-up costs
- Fast product launch built in
- Great for all types of projects
- Comprehensive *agile* package

Scrum's weaknesses

- Needs an *agile* mindset to flourish

Scrum needs a more considered launch but it's usually the best route in. It's easy enough to get to grips with the mechanics and has its own built-in checks to keep things humming.

It would be a mistake to simply see *Kanban* as a soft option, or as a stepping stone to *Scrum*. There are pros and cons, but both are rich in their own rights. There are times when there's a migration from one framework to the other but it happens both ways. It's certainly not one-way traffic.

Beware *agile* framework tripwires!

Agile frameworks offer a risk-free route in, plus it's inexpensive to get up and running (especially true with *Kanban* and *Scrum*). But things can go wrong and there are booby traps to be avoided:

- **Leaping before looking**: Avoid the temptation to dive in too early – think first and then plan. With *Kanban* it doesn't take much, so there's no excuse.

- **Selective implementation**: Take great care about using selective elements of any framework and be aware that the returns will be severely diminished.

- **Changing horses in mid-stream**: Teams do switch between *Kanban* and *Scrum* but constantly going backwards and forwards is far too disruptive.

- **It's all so obvious**: Don't be fooled into thinking the simplicity of *Kanban* and the straightforwardness of *Scrum* mean they're easy to get right. Plenty are discovering it needs a deft touch.

The final word

- -

Making the leap into the world of *agile* doesn't need to be risky or costly. Using a framework means the methods are crystal clear and allows everyone to focus on getting the implementation spot on. There are plenty of options but if you want a fast, seamless start then look no further than *Kanban* and *Scrum*. It really is a no-brainer.

Kanban is a great way to get a foot in the door. It's easy to understand and simplicity itself to use. It's nigh on impossible to get wrong, so there's no good reason for not at least having a crack for a few weeks, is there? And even though it's an easy, low-cost entry point, *Kanban* isn't a compromise solution and is perfectly capable of sparking a revolution.

Then there's *Scrum*, a veritable tour de force that is close to being perfectly formed. Although it can handle pretty much anything, it comes into its own with projects. There's a bit more to mastering the how-to-do mechanics and it pays to prepare but it's nothing to worry about. It's a comprehensive package that will not let you down.

If there are any lingering doubts about *agile*, then trying out one of these two is an inexpensive, low-risk way to test the water and dispel those fears. Even contemplating an implementation is guaranteed to generate rich material about how your world functions right now.

Go *agile* in an hour

Kick off with personal *Kanban*

It can be difficult to get the nod for the first *agile* project. Even in the most receptive organisations it can take a bit of time to get the ducks lined up and that can be frustrating. Well, during that (hopefully short) hiatus, try *Kanban* out for yourself. Use it to take to-do lists on to a whole different level.

Is there anyone in the world who doesn't use to-do lists? There are those of us who are drowning in a sea of the little buggers at times. Perhaps you have the self-discipline to only create one a day and religiously finish off everything before knocking off. Or maybe they're all over the place, both short and long but all half-finished.

Create a *Kanban* board, either one for work tasks or one for personal stuff. Whichever you prefer. For the best results use a workflow app like Trello, but it's fine to keep it simple for the purposes of this exercise – a sheet of flipchart paper and Post-it notes is about as low-tech as it gets. Then step through the following to get started:

1 Create tasks and stories – all with a specific, tangible outcome.

2 Prioritise them – shuffle them into an order of importance.

3 Set a WIP limit – set the maximum number of concurrent items.

4 Pull the first one – when complete then repeat.

Don't be tempted to set a high WIP limit as it defeats the object of the exercise. Settle on two or three at the most to begin with. Think about how your own operating practices can be improved. What are the blockers? Are there any tweaks which might make life easier? If you can't think of anything at all, you're not looking hard enough.

If handled correctly, this is nothing like a normal to-do list. The differences are subtle but significant. And as this is personal Kanban, continuing the journey is totally under your control.

chapter 6

More support from other *agile resources*

"You shouldn't go through life with a catcher's mitt on both hands. You need to be able to throw something back."

Maya Angelou

A sneak preview of Chapter 6

There's an unparalleled array of support and other useful resources on tap within the *agile* community, much of which is completely free:

- **International organisations**: With guidance, training, conferences and much more beside only a click away.

- **On-line discussion groups**: Plenty to choose from but with LinkedIn consistently a premium destination for all things *agile*.

- **Likeminded soulmates**: Face-to-face *MeetUps* offering wide ranging interest group and often free pizza too.

- **Training, mentoring and coaching**: If funds are available, a wide range of expert guidance is on offer.

A little help from your friends

Even though the basics are easy enough to grasp, there'll be plenty of questions along the way about the nuances. Like many other things, there's plenty of devil in the detail. The good news is there's an awe-inspiring range of support available, much of which is completely free. Covering anything from the general stuff asked at the start of the journey to specific issues raised by more experienced practitioners.

There's a sense of community within the *agile* world that feels almost evangelical at times because of the passion and devotion to the cause. Everything from non-profit organisations dedicated to spreading the word, right through to a long list of open social media-based forums chewing the cud about everything under the sun. Openness is very much the byword.

Paid-for stuff is on offer too, with plenty of training and expert advice to be found. *Agile* has become such big business that there are occasional rogues to contend with, as might be expected. A few organisations with debateable credentials and a growing band of false prophets claiming to be coaches. *Caveat emptor*, as it does pay to look before leaping.

But with a few notable exceptions, the cross-section of resources on tap is something exceptional. It's always a big bonus when expert advice is widely available, and that's especially true with *agile*. It means the right type of help is never far away, to help save time, heartache and even hard cash.

Visit an information hub

Discovering *agile* is a bit like hitting any new exciting place. It's enjoyable to wander around and explore topics that spark an interest and the web is a great source of information. For a fast start, there are several information hubs hosted by organisations that know their onions and whose sole purpose is to support the cause.

It's a measure of the success story that there are a growing number of well-established bodies dotted around the globe offering all sorts of support and resources. They're a magnet for anyone interested in the subject and are a great source of pre-vetted, reliable subject matter information, plus a hell of a lot more, including training and conferences.

It might be argued that the biggest and the best general-purpose destination is the Agile Alliance. In its own words it's 'a non-profit organization with global membership, committed to advancing *agile* development principles and practices'. At around $100 for an individual membership, and at least half that per head for the corporate route, it's good value. The annual conference is an *agile* showcase.

There are many fans of the *Scrum* Alliance and *Scrum*.org too. Both are unsurprisingly *Scrum*-centric, which is a bit of an advantage if it's the framework of choice, but they're broad churches anyway. They offer membership as part of their certification package and a basic membership too. Once again, their resources are a big draw and there's a huge community on tap.

All are very safe bets and well worth the price of admission. There are completists who join them all but one is normally enough. Admittedly, not everyone is a fan and there are a few fissures appearing in the communities recently. But this is an almost inevitable result of exponential growth, not because of fundamental flaws.

Checkout *agile* gurus

Members of the community are usually quite modest with countless unsung heroes. But there are many characters who are considered to be the keepers of the flame and it's well worth paying attention to what the gurus have to say. It's impossible to pin down a Top 10 but there are certain characters who are well worth keeping an eye on. *Agile* is continually evolving and it's a great way to keep in touch with new ideas.

Go *agile* in 15 minutes

Get to know the experts

Whether it's books, blogs, podcasts, advice or lectures, the *agile* glitterati have it all covered. As you might expect, full use is made of all the traditional channels and of social media. There is a technology bias but that has improved dramatically over recent years.

Listing all the influencers of note would be an impossible mission. Ditto to selecting the chart toppers. So instead here's a selection of varied characters to check out. There's a sound-bite with each one which is far from definitive but might whet your appetite:

Esther Derby – respected advocate of teamwork and *Retrospectives*

Roman Pichler – leading light on all things *Product Owner* related

Mike Cohn – widely known and respected *agile* beacon

Lyssa Adkins – respected coach and best-selling author

David Anderson – key player in the *Kanban* community

Jeff Sutherland – co-founder of *Scrum* and a leading authority

Craig Larman – leading authority on *scaling agile*

Mary Poppendieck – popular *Lean* thinker and advocate

Ken Schwaber – occasionally controversial co-founder of *Scrum*

Henrik Kniberg – wide-ranging expertise and popular author

Some might argue Mike Cohn is the leader of the pack, but others point to the heritage of Mary Poppendieck. But the knowledge and engaging style of Henrik Kniberg takes some beating. Whenever you have 15 minutes to spare, pick one of them at random and check them out.

Find *agile* soulmates

There's nothing more productive and fun than hooking up with like-minded people to shoot the breeze. Openly sharing experiences, both good and bad, is very much part of the *agile* ethos. Talking to colleagues is part of the daily regime but there's much to be gained from exposure to people outside the inner circle. An excellent place to seek out new soulmates and tap into their experiences is at www.meetup.com.

Meetup.com is a social networking site that allows you to find and join groups related to your own personal interests. However, instead of just talking about these interests online, Meetup.com is used to organise face-to-face get-togethers with a broad agenda. There are meet-ups for all sorts of mainstream and niche subjects including anything from mountaineering to stamp collecting. It will come as no surprise that *agile* groups are flourishing and there's very likely to be one within striking distance.

There's no standard format for *agile* meet-ups and that's part of the attraction. Some are regular but many others convene infrequently, some stick to a trusted itinerary but many prefer to experiment. However, the common denominator is far more important: individuals with a passion for the subject looking to share their thoughts and ideas with their peers. The formula is very *agile* in its own right and checking out a few sessions is highly recommended.

Quite often there are guest speakers or set topics to discuss. Some even post sample videos, and looking back over recent material is bound to give you a feel. The best bits are before or after the main event when people mingle freely and discuss whatever they fancy. It's a brilliant opportunity, especially if there are *agile* things on your mind.

Sessions are frequented by a mixed bunch with a variety of experiences to share and a welcoming, friendly vibe is the de facto norm. *Agile* hasn't reached the point where there's the equivalent of a tourist information office in every major city but this is the next best thing.

Go *agile* in 15 minutes

Watch a YouTube video

There are plenty of snappy videos available and YouTube is a good source. Here's a couple of 15-minute suggestions as a taster:

- **Intro to *Kanban* in Under 5 Minutes (What is *Kanban*, Learn *Kanban*) and Intro to *Scrum* in Under 10 Minutes:** There are numerous videos summarising these tricky subjects in no time at all. These two are well known and respected.

- ***Agile* Product Ownership in a Nutshell by Henrik Kniberg:** As an example of top-notch material, check out this 15-minute animated presentation. It's a one-day product ownership course compressed into a quarter of an hour. Widely considered to be superb.

  If you do decide to have an independent scoot around the web then be careful as you'll soon find that it's a very mixed bag. You may need to kiss a few frogs.

Be *agile* on a beach

Sticking with the theme of linking up with like-minded souls, there are opportunities to take it up a notch from meet-ups with specialist, dedicated gatherings that last a full day or more. Some are called workshops, while others are dubbed conferences, but these handles do not adequately convey what's on offer when the *agile* community organises a get-together. Let's take a closer look at a fine example.

Surely it was a moment of pure genius when 'Agile On The Beach' was set up. It's a conference and it's staged in a beautiful location in Falmouth, Cornwall – the promo shots would do any holiday brochure proud. The *MVP* launched in 2011 with help but now it's self-sustaining. Its grown to 50 plus speakers and sessions spanning two days, with over 400 gathering to explore the latest thinking within the community.

Check out www.agileonthebeach.com to find out more or dip into any of the typical social media outlets such as its YouTube channel. Getting people to interact and share experiences is the key to success, and it's a recurring *agile* theme that there's nothing wrong with enjoying what you do. Although this event is special, it's worth searching for other gatherings near to home. Standard rules apply and there's no need to get clever: search for *agile*, conference and the closest decent-sized town is more than enough.

Agile tips

In search of the best get-togethers

It's well known that until recently IT was leading the charge but now there's plenty of non-techie interest as well. Even schools and the medical profession are developing an interest. *Agile* is everywhere in various shapes, forms and guises. Keep an open mind.

One of the finest, somewhat unexpected, sources of *agile* material and contacts is the annual QA&TEST Conference on Embedded Software Testing in Bilbao, Spain. Quite a mouthful but it's a masterpiece of organisation and in a great location – it attracts all the rights sorts. Highly recommended even if you know nothing about embedded software testing – and there are plenty of us in that boat.

Keep an open mind. Even mixing with the anti-agile lobby can be a rich source of learning as they usually have a bad experience to share. It's useful to test your faith.

Join a group

Maybe joining an organisation, popping along to a meet-up, or diving into a beachside conference feels a bit too much? If so, a much gentler entry point is to check out one of the many excellent *agile* social media-based discussion groups. There's plenty to choose from and all the decent ones have public profiles to check out and reply to polite enquiries. Quite often the group name alone is usually enough to gauge the content.

A welcoming *agile* vibe is guaranteed. Plenty of like-minded people with shared interests, hallmarked by an incredible generosity and openness. There's a sympathetic ethos and nothing seems too much trouble – even when topics have been around the block a few times before. At times it's hard to believe how closely the detail is scrutinised in discussion threads and the best posts generate a fantastic cross-section of feedback.

There are a number of popular destinations but it's hard to go wrong with LinkedIn. It's well known as an excellent all-round information hub and it's especially well geared up to the world of *agile*. Articles and think-pieces representing the latest thinking are widely available, and the discussion groups are excellent, especially for newcomers. LinkedIn is a highly effective way to launch into *agile* groups.

These days all professionals are *expected* to have a LinkedIn account but if you've been working from a remote island until recently, then sign up for a free account straightaway at www. linkedin.com and take it from there.

Go *agile* in 15 minutes

Join a LinkedIn group

LinkedIn is a rich and diverse source of *agile* material, especially the discussion groups. It doesn't take much to sign up and nobody sensible gets turned down – the more the merrier is the ethos. There's a little bit of extra prep required if you don't have a LinkedIn account and factor in a short time lapse before becoming an active member.

Once in, start off by plugging *Agile* or *Scrum* or *Kanban* into the group search. You'll get a vast list to choose from such as the grand-sounding *Scrum Masters* or the intriguing *Kanban to Improve the World*. If you're happy with an initial recommendation or just feeling lazy then opt for *Scrum Practitioners*.

Common sense applies when assessing groups. Even if *Agile Belarus* is more exclusive, a large membership base tends to provide better overall coverage. There's never any pressure to join in the chats so it's easy to sit back, observe and pick up tips. The exchanges are nearly always educational and occasionally hilarious.

The number of posts in a chat is a useful filter – anything with over 50 responses has clearly sparked a very lively debate and is worth checking out.

No *agile* stone is ever left unturned in the best groups and get ready to witness passionate discussions over apparently light subjects. Don't be afraid to post a question – these are frequented by the most inclusive and forgiving people in town – but be streetwise. Asking for training recommendations is a perennial favourite that usually generates decent advice but expect the vultures to start circling too.

Agile in action

Small budget, big ambitions

AgileParcs invested in copies of this book for everyone in the organisation to ensure they all knew the basics and started on roughly the same page (no pun intended).

With *Scrum* as their framework of choice, the team saw joining the Agile Alliance as a good route to plenty of useful material. Two cemented their knowledge by going through related material on YouTube. Others dipped into the free online training material but were a bit disappointed in the quality and quickly abandoned that ship.

Everyone dived into groups in LinkedIn with varying success. Overall the feedback was positive, but a recurring complaint was the number of posters with their own agendas. Swapping examples of invaluable tips and crazy comments became a popular feature on team nights out.

With no *agile* meet-ups in the area, the AgileParcs team decided to host their own. Being sited in a beautiful location helped attract a decent crowd to the inaugural event. One of the lessons learned was to be optimistic and buy more sausages for the barbeque.

Going to the next Agile Alliance conference in North America was met with a frosty response from the CEO who countered with letting one of the team go to Agile On The Beach. The team voted almost unanimously on who to send.

Big ambitions don't need a big budget.

Getting ready to launch

Chances are you won't be on a solo operation and an extended crew needs to be brought up to speed. If so, even with a tried and trusted framework plus guidance from a decent book, it's never plain sailing when launching on a bigger scale. It pays dividends to draft in an expert, a coach, to guarantee a smooth lift-off. It's cheaper to go the DIY route but that's usually a false economy as there are tripwires to negotiate.

Coaching is a very broad term and at times it seems like everyone and their dog is claiming to have these skills. It can be quite a challenge to find one who fits the bill and with whom you feel a rapport. It's a bit like finding the right doctor or dentist, and it's best to ask around first as recommendations are worth their weight in gold. Usually somebody knows somebody who knows somebody.

There's an extensive range of independent coaches available (not all with dogs) and a reasonable smattering of organisations that offer a wide range of training services:

- **Basic training**: Typically a group induction before lift-off but can be run when the need arises post-launch. A general *agile* primer can also be beneficial to those outside the main line of fire. These tend to be non-framework specific and focus on more general themes such as the benefits of collaborating in small teams. Often as little as a half day and never more than one.

- **Certified training**: Usually this is specific to the job role or framework, such as a primer for *Product Management* or the basics of *Scrum* Mastery. The value of these is a hot potato and many believe they aren't great investments. If money isn't an issue, they're certainly worth considering. Usually a minimum of a couple of days in duration.

- **Tailored training**: It's easy to get basic or certified training tailored to an organisation's specific requirements. The core material will be bog-standard, but the nuances and examples can be more targeted. The same duration can be expected but minimum quotas of six to eight people are the norm and expect to pay a bit more per head to cover the customisation.

- **Developmental support**: Once the journey begins, it pays dividends to reinforce good habits and keep everyone on message. This is most effective when it involves the whole team to really drill into the detail of being *agile*. In the aftermath of a launch it's well worth having a day of coaching here and there with the frequency diminishing over time.

- **Doctor's surgery**: Independent health checks guarantee that no serious malaise develops into a lifestyle-threatening condition. Best executed by observing the whole team in action, but it can focus on specific individuals if really necessary. This can be incorporated into the developmental support sessions or whenever there's an unexpected *agile* crisis.

- **Relationship counselling**: *Agile* is a people business and passions sometimes run high, so it's not surprising that personal spats occur that benefit from counselling. At times this is merely about offering a sounding board to air frustrations but more often it's for long-term run-ins or when a team is dysfunctional for no obvious reason. This is very much on-demand.

- **One-off specials**: There are times when it pays to bring in a specialist facilitator for an event or with an end product in mind. The most popular slot is when developing the *Team Charter*. The outcome needs to be on the money and an experienced, independent facilitator makes all the difference. As and when needed of course.

Building a flexible working relationship with a coach is important. At times your needs will be wide ranging and intense and at other times a light touch will suffice. Aim to establish a link-up early on, preferably even before lift-off. If the budget allows, get a coach in to deliver an *agile* primer for everyone and see them in action. If all goes well, appropriate follow-up sessions can be organised.

Agile tips

Formal training options

Despite the polarised views about formal training, it's worth considering, especially if the budget allows. On a personal level, there's no doubt that certification looks good on the CV and some recruiters see it as a must-have. The experience itself is short and sweet: meet nice people, learn a bit about *agile* and get the T-shirt.

- *Certified or non-certified*: Certified training gets you a recognised qualification and non-certified doesn't. Certification tends to be more expensive and is less flexible regarding content – you just follow the syllabus. Certified tends to look more impressive on the CV but there are better non-licensed courses available if you look hard enough.

- *Public or private*: A private course is run in-house and there's much more flexibility about who, what and when. Although these can be certified they tend to be used for tailored material. A public course is a scheduled event, commonly held at a training venue and anyone can book on to it. Public certified courses tend to have wider appeal.

Accredited courses are much of a muchness in terms of content, but some trainers know their onions and some just know the course material. As with everything agile-related, a recommendation helps.

The *agile* community is knee-deep with coaches these days but finding the right one can be a mighty struggle. Asking if anyone can recommend a great one in a LinkedIn group is an option but expect the vultures to start hovering. Personal endorsements based on experience are definitely a better option and this is one area where MeetUp contacts can come in particularly useful.

There are specialist coaching/training organisations around that offer an array of options in terms of material and resources. But there's much to be said for building up a relationship with an independent. There are pros and cons. The best solo artists will never be available on demand, whereas dealing with a company may mean dealing with more than one person.

Whatever the source, be a bit wary of anyone without hands-on experience in the past few years.

Agile in action

AgileParcs links up with a coach

After getting off to a flying start on a tiny budget, the AgileParcs team became frustrated at times. It wasn't always practical to rely on LinkedIn to answer all their specific questions and provide other guidance. It was agreed that a bit of coaching was worth considering.

Unfortunately, the whizz who helped with the charter wasn't available. Luckily one of the regular faces at their local meet-up recommended contacting a company called *Agility in Mind*. Ed Scotcher came in the following week and proposed a short series of fortnightly coaching sessions to begin with.

Ed sat in on various team events to get the lie of the land and initially worked closely with their *Product Manager* and *Scrum Master* who were both struggling to keep up. The improvements were tweaks for the most part, but there were a couple of specifics. After the first batch of six support sessions, AgileParcs moved on to quarterly check-ups.

The AgileParcs CEO admitted to having concerns about the cost but quickly realised the sessions were self-funding. Improved productivity, plus having a much happier gang, more than justified the expense. The underpinning ethos at *Agility in Mind* – that delivery is everything – went a long way to calming the nerves.

Agility in Mind set the bar nice and high without over-complicating what was on offer. Although one-off sessions are available, they much preferred to think in terms of building a deeper relationship – a simple formula that worked well for AgileParcs.

Agility in Mind is a real agile consultancy offering a wide range of services. It works with the AgileParcs of this world and a diverse bunch of others.

Bargain basement training

Apart from the polished, highly professional courses on offer, there's a shed load of inexpensive web-based *agile* training available too. Low-cost repositories such as www.lynda.com and www.udemy. com offer more courses than anyone could possibly find the time to watch. There are two big advantages: primarily cheap as chips and easy to dip into.

If you already have access to the subscription-based www.lynda. com then it's a no-brainer to try out a couple of courses. But there's no highly rated *agile* material getting rave reviews and the same applies to www.udemy.com. So before signing up for a £12.99 bargain (usually down from £199.99 and only available for another 12 hours), ask yourself: is it the course content that is attractive or the price?

Although it generally pays to be wary of bargain basement online training, there are a few exceptions. For example, it's well worth checking out www.scrumtrainingseries.com. It's free and watching the whole shooting match will only require an investment of about two hours, plus thinking time. There's a slight IT slant but nothing to stress about – not a bad way to while away a spare evening.

'Definitely not convinced' is an expression that springs to mind here. The best of the material is OK but that's hardly a ringing endorsement. Far better to explore the other resources we've covered elsewhere. Be especially wary of anything on sale more often than DFS furniture.

Beware *agile* resource tripwires!

The support and other resources freely available within the *agile* community is one of the jewels in the crown. But there are inherent dangers and bear traps to avoid falling into:

- **Endless hours surfing**: The breadth of material out there is staggering so be very careful. It's very easy to whittle away hours binge viewing and ending up no wiser.

- **False prophets**: Every man, woman and their dogs seem to be *agile* coaches and mentors these days. Choose your guides carefully and always look for recommendations.

- **Spoilt for choice**: Whatever you're looking for, the breadth of options available can be overpowering. Be careful to avoid endless procrastination about every move.

- **Debating societies**: Discussion groups are a fantastic source of ideas and advice but have an occasional tendency to put too much focus on theory rather than outcomes.

- **Different opinions**: Given the nature of *agile*, it's inevitable for people to have different takes on points of detail. Celebrate differences, don't go to war over next-to-nothing.

The final word

One of the biggest attractions of *agile* is the negligible entry cost of joining the club. No expensive membership charges, no up-front license fees and no hidden running costs. Getting up to speed can be done for next to nothing if the budget is extremely tight – with diverse and wide-ranging resources freely available. If there's a bit of cash to splash, even more options open up.

Excellent subject matter reading material is available, for the most part openly shared. A grounding can be achieved with a laptop, access to the internet and an inquisitive mind. Forums are widely available, and the community prides itself on supporting fellow travellers. Meet-ups are out there offering subject matter expertise and often free nosh too.

Be a bit wary of operating on a zero budget as corners can be cut when there's cash to invest wisely. *Agile* looks very easy to do, but as many DIYers confess, it's often worth getting an expert along to provide a helping hand when the time is right, or the need is great. Think about the benefits of getting coaching, at least on a limited basis.

Another note of caution: the biggest danger is of spending too much time preparing to fly, which isn't very *agile* at all. As with learning to ride a bike, there comes a point where enough is enough and you need to jump on to the saddle.

Go *agile* in an hour

Join the Agile Alliance (for free)

When it comes to looking at resource-rich, inclusive and well-respected organisations, the Agile Alliance is right up there. As an added bonus it offers a free Agile Alliance Subscriber membership which is an excellent try-before-you-buy option and more than enough initially.

Once signed up, the best place to begin is checking out the various *Agile Essential* sections. There's a danger of spending the whole hour there but move on to check out the vast array of resources and events material on offer. With plenty more besides, the allotted time may not be enough.

There is a techie slant to some of the material and the organisation itself but that's true of the whole movement. The Agile Alliance is truly international but with a bit of a US bias, so don't expect its next annual conference to be up the road from you. Unless of course you happen to be reading this in Denver, Colorado.

A full individual membership is available for $99 with the usual discounts for mass sign-ups. But plenty get by on the freebie.

---

chapter 7

Light the fuse

"You won't get better at playing the piano by running around the piano."

José Mourinho

A sneak preview of Chapter 7

Agile Now contains everything you need, whatever the next step is and here's some last-minute, pre-flight, Go *Agile* think-pieces:

- **Go for it**: There's everything to gain and nothing to lose, so here are the final tips for a quick launch.
- **Get regular health checks**: Ways to keep an eye on your *agile* health and guarantee a risk-free lifestyle.
- **Options for a wider rollout**: How to scale up your *agile* operations, or to even go Big Bang from the beginning.
- **Emergency contact details**: What to do if there are any lingering doubts, queries or suggestions.

Get cracking

There are plenty of good reasons for picking up a book like this. Perhaps you're thinking of going *agile* soon and on the lookout for guidance. Maybe you're already on the path and eyeing ways to become even *better and faster*. Or you're possibly curious and wanting to know a little bit more about this topical topic. Might even be cramming for a hot job interview!

The aim of *Agile Now* is to set you up to kick on, whatever the intended destination. To provide a solid understanding of the basics and guidance for where to go if there are any lingering doubts. It might be necessary to read through the book again, check out a LinkedIn group or go to a couple more meet-ups but if you've read all this with due care and attention, you'll be fine.

Agile has something for everyone when used sensibly. It's a magic mixture of innovative ideas, proven thinking and basic common sense. The recent explosion of interest is well deserved – the direct result of brilliant success stories and great word-of-mouth. It isn't a miracle cure, but *Kanban* and *Scrum* offer proven ways to make that dream come true. If there's a need – and there usually is – there's absolutely no reason to stall.

We're all in search of *cheaper, faster, better* in one form or other. Especially better. Go *agile!*

Go for it

If pure curiosity or a tasty job opportunity was the driver behind buying this book, then it should be job done by now. But it's more likely the reason was related to more complex matters about going *agile* or with issues mid-stream. So let's talk about those situations a bit more. If you're about to set off, then factor in this guidance and if you're already moving then double-check you've acted on it already.

Once the decision is made to go for it, the exciting question is how to start. A very popular and simple option is to pilot *agile* on a suitable chunk of work – this is by far the most popular first step. Another, much more ambitious approach is to get the whole organisation to go for it big time – and for obvious reasons this doesn't happen often. Or if all else fails there's the option for personal *agile* – not the preferred choice but great trees grow from small acorns.

Whatever the backdrop, treat going *agile* as a venture in its own right. Yes, the end game may be very different – ranging from personal to corporate *agility* – but the basic premise is going to be the same. As with any new strategic endeavour, begin by defining the end game or the *Vision* as we now know it. Pin down exactly what you want to achieve. Often, it's more than a project, it's a passion.

Once the *Vision* is in place, build a *Backlog* and then, hey, you're off. Of course, there'll be a big difference in the detail between kicking off a *Kanban* board for the family chores compared to introducing *Scrum* into a FTSE 100 organisation, but the fundamentals are the same.

Agile in action

AgileParcs goes *agile*

One of the key players at AgileParcs had the experience of using a *Kanban* board for all the family to-do jobs outside of work. Each had a snappy title, a full description and a view on how big the job was based on T-shirts sizes (S, M, L, XL and XXL). Tasks were loaded up on to the Trello app whenever a new one sprung to mind.

This *Backlog* was prioritised based on a mix of family pressure, but there was a tendency to pick up the quick wins when the time available was tight. There was a house rule that no more than two jobs could be on the go at any one time, except in emergency situations when more were allowed to avoid tantrums.

From these humble beginnings, the use of *Kanban* crept into the AgileParcs organisation. Based on reading, it was agreed to adopt *Scrum* for the bulk of the main site development. A decision was taken to spend time setting up the framework properly in a series of one-week *Sprints* to deliver the following:

- **Sprint 1**: The AgileParcs *Vision* and initial *Backlog* – defining the *Vision* was workshop-based and a relatively straightforward, one *User Story* activity. Building the *Backlog* was broken down into a series of other loosely connected tasks.

- **Sprint 2**: Roles and responsibilities – assigning roles and responsibilities based on the *Scrum* framework was relatively straightforward too but the lack of a suitable *Scrum Master* became evident. This led to several follow-ups culminating in a new recruit to the organisation.

- **Sprint 3**: *Team Charter* and support tools – AgileParcs wanted to get this spot on and partnered up with a recommended coach. The final version of the charter was in the form of a huge visual glossy thanks to a local print company.

Putting the foundation stones in place helped to solidify the values, mindset and supporting practices – and it all happened in less than a month. Theirs is a common entry point, and it always pays dividends to have a structured *agile* launch. Initial planning doesn't need to be over-egged, so resist the temptation to dive straight into the deep end.

It's very tempting to roll up your sleeves and get cracking with the real graft, but it pays to set yourself up for success.

Get regular health checks

The constant search for improvements is baked into the normal regime and plays a prominent part in all the leading frameworks. It's useful to supplement this, by scheduling in other occasional independent spot checks just in case. Even the finest athletes at the peak of their powers get themselves checked out by specialists on a periodic basis.

It pays to do this even when things appear to be going swimmingly well and you're operating within the protection of frameworks. *Kanban* and *Scrum* are brilliant but there's still a danger of bad practice slowly creeping in. It's surprising how many experienced teams veer off track occasionally despite the in-built protection.

Here are three simple-to-implement health checks that can be used on a regular or irregular basis. They can be random events without prior warning or included as a commitment in the *Team Charter*. All can be self-administered but for maximum effect get an independent observer, such as a coach, to drive.

Testing the team temperature at the daily gathering

This is a simple check and should be a daily, almost subconscious, review by every member of the team anyway. But once in a while get a second opinion from a friendly face outside of the team. The *Daily Kanban*, *Daily Scrum* or *Daily Stand-Up* format is extremely straightforward to follow and everyone plays their part in keeping to the script. Problems here are like a high temperature and need to be investigated – quite often a minor blip and a false alarm but it can be an early warning of something serious.

- What's the regularity? The only acceptable answer is at the same time every normal working day without fail.
- Is the agreed format always used? Focussing on what was done yesterday, plans for today and any blockers.
- Are the team paying attention? This is an update for their benefit, not a status report for the *Scrum Master*.
- What happens with the blockers? They must be noted and acted on immediately afterwards.

Stand-Ups follow a blisteringly simple format but of course there'll be deviations occasionally – times when a key issue can be discussed and sorted in a couple of minutes with all the team there. But be careful to avoid too many exceptions to the rule. And be wary if certain individuals repeatedly transgress by always looking to duck out or are reluctant to contribute when there.

Checking the blood pressure at the *Retrospectives*

Getting the best out of *Retrospectives* is a crucial part of the *agile* ethos so it pays to step back occasionally and reflect on them directly. Not only to confirm they're running well with the expected outcomes being churned out, but also to check the team are not feeling too much heat. This is a precautionary examination to ensure there's enough pressure to inspire results but no risk of heart failure.

- Is everyone chipping in? Everyone should contribute at least one thing of consequence.

- Are there clear outcomes? An occasional moan-fest is acceptable, but the norm needs to be actions rather than hot air.

- How many things done well are mentioned? Expect at least a regular trickle of positive comments.

- Are the same observations re-occurring? Good, bad and ugly points must all be acted on, not noted and then forgotten about.

Whatever the format in the *Retrospectives*, expect them to focus on: *what do we do well* and *what can we do better?* Of course, it's OK if the team needs to let off steam from time to time but the general vibe needs to stay upbeat, continually in a search for tweaks and improvements. Loud alarm bells should be ringing if there's little of lasting value generated, especially if sessions are consistently degenerating into the blame game.

Full end-to-end annual reviews

The team will always have a gut feel for how things are going but put time aside for a full annual check-up. This should include a look at the *Daily Stand-Ups* and another *Retrospective* of *Retrospectives*, but centre stage is a review of the *Team Charter*. As with any deeper dive, target this to happen annually but don't be afraid to bring it forward if any concerns or other warning signs are spotted.

- Is the charter a living document? This shouldn't be the first visit since inception, so expect the team to have it constantly in mind.
- Do the team live by the spirit of the rules? Occasional blips are natural but be concerned about any outright disrespect or regular disregard.
- Any improvements recommended? It's impossible to nail down a perfect, positive culture, so the *Team Charter* must evolve over time.

If the Stand-Ups are going well, the *Retrospectives* are constantly sparking improvements and the *Team Charter* is a living document then put yourselves forward for Agile Team of The Year. In reality, perfect teams are unheard of but if any or all of those areas are very weak then there may be trouble brewing.

All checks can be self-administered but it's invariably more effective to get an independent assessment (a decent coach should be keeping an eye on these key indicators anyway). Act on issues early and don't be tempted to ignore any symptoms of ill health. If caught early, anything can be fixed, but left to fester it might be terminal.

Go *agile* in 15 minutes

Buy an off-piste book

It's surprisingly easy to get caught up in the excitement and it can start to feel like everything is about hard core *agile*. All work and no play can make you very dull, so it's important to make time for life's little pleasures. Luckily you can be entertained and be mentally challenged by one of these little bit off-piste books:

Grit by Angela Duckworth: Why passion and resilience are the secrets to success delivered with good humour. No surprise this was a #1 Sunday Times bestseller.

The Coaching Habit by Michael Bungay Stanier: How to say less, ask more and change the way you operate forever. Practical, game-changing advice.

Black Box Thinking by Matthew Syed: How great perform-
ers and teams are driven by an insatiable search for marginal
gains. Learning from mistakes with hard-hitting examples.

The Chimp Paradox by Steve Peters: A mind management
model that can promote health, happiness and success. Get to
grips with the complex subject of how your brain works.

*Go into a bookshop and read the first few pages of each one.
You might end up buying them all. Off piste and fun to read
but complimentary.*

Teams working in multiple locations

With *agile* there's a definite preference for teams to be co-located.
Working together as a self-contained, empowered team is far easier
when everyone is literally sitting side by side. In fact, there was even
a time when this was seen as a non-negotiable prerequisite. However, co-location isn't always viable and over recent years there's
been an acceptance of *Distributed Teams* spread across multiple geo-
graphical locations.

There are also times when *working from home* is a neces-
sity. Anything from a child-minding emergency, a planned rail
strike, extreme weather conditions or an unexpected pandemic.
This can affect some or all of the team and may be a one-off or a
long-standing situation to deal with. Whatever the backdrop is,
keeping the conversations and collaboration flowing is always a
challenge when folk are spread out.

It will come as no surprise that technology plays a significant part in
helping a team stay connected when they're based in multiple locations.
This is largely achieved by utilising tech solutions that are freely
available, portable and easy to set up at the drop of a hat if necessary:

Questions: Messaging is an extremely effective way to ask and answer
questions. All the widely used apps, such as *Slack or WhatsApp,* cater for
a direct one-to-one approach or a group exchange.

Chats: Video conference calling is the most commonly used substitute when a face-to-face is impossible. Messaging apps offer this feature too or there are dedicated options.

Meetings: When a larger crowd is involved and the format is more structured, the likes of *MS Teams* and *Zoom* offer plenty of bells and whistles to keep good order, share information and promote inclusivity.

Task Management: There's plenty of choice when it comes to software dedicated to managing an *agile* workflow. *Trello* and *Jira* are fully featured and have big fan bases in the *agile* community.

Look at what's on offer with *MS Office 365* or *Google G* Suite as they're both excellent benchmarks for the *must have* facilities for communicating and collaborating remotely. Quite possibly you're already using bits 'n bobs from one of them! Either one, alongside a specialised *agile* workflow management tool such as *Trello* or *Jira*, helps get the best out of people working in multiple locations.

Agile in action
AgileParcs and Covid-19

After Covid-19 hit, the AgileParcs team worked from home for a considerable period and technology played a significant part in their day-to-day *agile* life. There was an explosion of messaging and video con calling with all sorts of software in use, based on personal preferences.

Eventually, by common consensus, the long list of acceptable options was whittled down to Slack and Zoom with a longer-term corporate plan of moving over to MS Teams. The superb banter on the all-team Slack channel played a major part in keeping everyone's spirits up.

Conference calling was used for all the *Daily Stand-Ups* and the physical wallboard was moved over to a *Jira* based electronic task board to track progress. To everyone's surprise, the *Stand-Ups* were tighter and more focussed with far fewer people just butting in.

When things eased up, the team came in again for important set-pieces such as *Sprint Planning* and *Retrospectives*. When restrictions relaxed even further, they went back to a more traditional set-up on the whole. But there was an almost unanimous preference for using an electronic task board and the wallboard was ditched permanently.

The messaging repartee became a permanent fixture and the team comms channel was the first thing to be set up after the migration to MS Teams.

Less is more

Our focus has been on getting the foundations right for a single, pilot implementation. But once there's an isolated success story there may well be an appetite for rolling it out further, maybe even across the whole organisation. There's no doubt about the benefits of having more people on the same page and it's a whole different ballgame when *agile* becomes the norm, with everyone sharing the same ways of working and mindset.

It's fair to say large-scale rollouts have a chequered history, especially Big Bang implementations. But even though some say *scaling* is the movement's Achilles heel, it has been done successfully many, many times. So, if there are ever grand designs on the horizon, spend time looking into the three best established and most widely acclaimed approaches.

Agile definitions
Scaling

Most *agile* launches are limited affairs, quite often a low-profile pilot project. Then once there's one or more successes, there will be much more interest in jumping on the bandwagon. Usually going from one team to two and then on to three, but occasionally the growth is more rapid, even exponential. *Scaling* is the process of going from wherever you begin to much wider usage.

Very few organisations are 100% agile but plenty are getting there, step by step.

SAFe (scaled *agile* framework)

SAFe is spreading rapidly around the world and is a huge commercial success story. It's also prone to generating heated arguments between the pro and anti factions. Seventy percent of Fortune 100 companies, and a growing number of the Global 2000, have certified SAFe professionals and consultants on site, and over 450,000 practitioners have been trained to date.

SAFe launched in 2011 and it's on a roll. If personal marketability is the prime objective, then it's a very safe bet (pun intended). There have been doubters from the very beginning, many with very strong opinions but there's no question it's the latest flavour of the month when it comes to *scaling*. See www.scaledagile.com for more comprehensive information.

LeSS (large-scale *Scrum*)

LeSS is a lightweight framework for *scaling Scrum* to more than one team. The big difference to other *scaling* frameworks is it provides a minimalistic framework that enables teams and organisations to *inspect and adapt* based on experience. *Agile* purists tend to *lean* towards this approach (pun intended again).

LeSS supporters argue that providing prescriptive *scaling* guidance for organisations to work within is fatally flawed. Instead, it recommends *scaling* frameworks should be bare bones with organisations allowed to fill in the detail. Check out www.less.works for more information.

The Spotify model

The amazing success story at music streaming company Spotify has generated many wannabes and copying its exact modus operandi is surprisingly popular. When people talk about the Spotify model what they mean is the way Spotify found to scale beyond the team to a larger organisation. Spotify teams mostly do something along the lines of *ScrumBan – Kanban* with some of the *Scrum Events* and other stuff thrown in as well.

The idea of organically developing an approach to *scaling* is a solid one and analysing the Spotify story is likely to spark ideas. But drawing on the experience of others is very different to apeing them. Copycatting the Spotify model might seem an attractive shortcut but be very careful as nuances that worked well for them are not likely to suit everyone. Better to come up with a personalised hybrid, pinching an idea from here and there before adding your own spin.

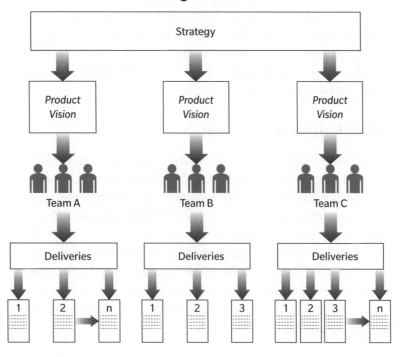

Scaling in action

Agile works brilliantly when there's one standalone team working in blissful isolation but life's more complicated when there are two, three or four teams – especially with the thorny challenge of inter-team coexistence, as illustrated by the diagram on the previous page. Imagine the complexity when the whole organisation is on the same journey but if Google and Spotify can pull it off, then so can you.

Tread carefully, yes. But remember a drive for a wider implementation is a positive step invariably on the back of one or more successes. It's not something to be feared.

Beware of *go agile* tripwires!

There might well be mixed feelings about going *agile*. It's normal to feel a bit nervous and to even have reservations. But be careful to mitigate against any emerging *anti-agile* sentiment with the potential to scupper the launch. These are the most common:

- *It's all so obvious:* It certainly is easy to grasp the gist, but the subtleties and nuances are harder to master. Don't underestimate the power and depth of simple ideas.

- *I do it because I have to:* Understanding the mechanics is the easy bit. It's getting into the right frame of mind that can be challenging. And one negative influencer needs dealing with before there's a ripple effect.

- *We already have Daily Stand-Ups:* There's much more to the full package than a 15-minute group huddle every day. It's an end-to-end way of working not a once-a-day event.

- *Some stuff isn't needed:* It's fine to debate the nuances but avoid ditching core practices. If certain aspects aren't quite working, then fix them – don't abandon them.

- *Great stuff but it's not for us:* Think very hard before throwing in the towel. Dig deeper into why and explore the underlying issues. Usually there are no real blockers, only self-generated excuses.

If anyone is convinced it's not going to work for them, then it definitely won't. Beware the prophets of doom as negative thinking can be infectious.

The final, final word

If you happen to have a very successful formula, then sticking with what you do right now is a pretty decent option. But it's only a serious choice in exceptional circumstances as most of us know there's always scope for improvements. The degree of opportunity will vary but there's usually ample room to become *cheaper, faster or better* – quite often all three.

Be wary if things aren't going well and you feel *agile* isn't the answer. Try to get to the root of why it isn't viable as this might provide vital clues about the wider malaise. Yes, change can be daunting but reflect on examples of once proud corporate dinosaurs who couldn't adapt to changing circumstances and became extinct. Think very carefully before putting this book to one side and soldiering on.

If you're in the same boat as the majority of us, there's work to be done. It might boil down to a series of small tweaks or perhaps a serious overhaul. *Agile* is here to help and can handle every eventuality. It provides a proven structure for getting stuff done more effectively and there are ready-made frameworks to help deliver. *Go agile!*

Go *agile* in an hour

Bedtime reading

If all has gone according to plan, by now you'll know exactly what you're going to do next. It might be to bite the bullet, with either a soft launch or an all guns blazing leap. Or, if the journey has already started, this could be the time to regroup and redouble the effort.

If you're serious about *agile* then please make sure you get a decent grounding. Reading this book cover to cover is one of the easiest options. It's not a massive tome and has everything you need to know to get underway.

Let's be honest, everybody is darn busy these days and there's a reasonable chance you've cut a few corners on the way to this point in the book. Perhaps dipped in and out. Possibly read selected chapters or maybe only checked out the first and last ones. But it's easy to catch up.

An hour a night for a couple of weeks should be enough. Or, even better, schedule a slot each day at work. This is not only good for you – it has the potential to be a big winner for the people around you and the organisation as a whole.

If there are any lingering doubts or concerns and you need a helping hand, then drop me an email at rob.cole@brilliantpm.co.uk. Always glad to help. And sincere apologies if you've already read the whole caboodle!

At the very, very least have a long hard think about the notes you made at the end of the first chapter and consider how going agile might help. There's something for everyone if you look close enough.

Index